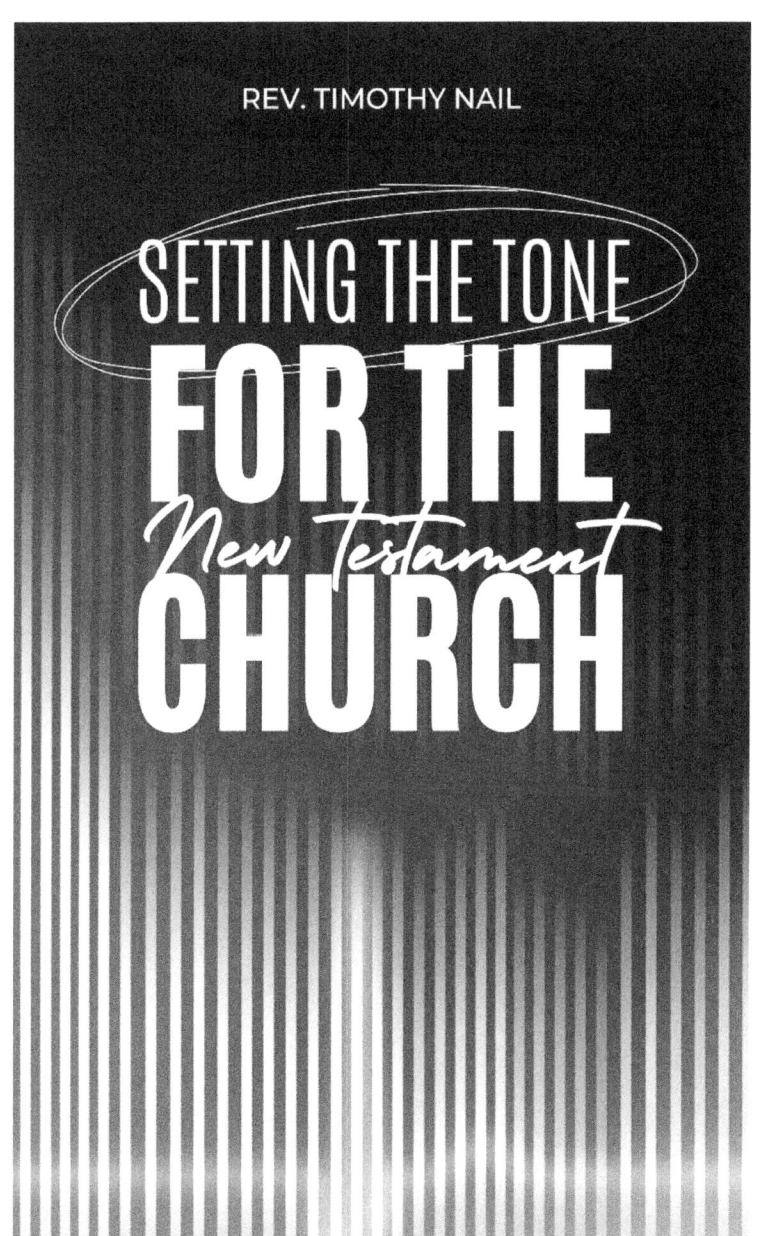

TABLE OF CONTENTS

Preface..*pg. 15*

Introduction..*pg. 17*

Chapter 1:
The Modern Pentecostal Church As I See It...............*pg. 23*

Chapter 2:
Peter's Message At Pentecost............................*pg. 41*

Chapter 3:
The Church Of Acts Was An Empowered Church.........*pg. 61*

Chapter 4:
The Church Of Acts Was An Enthroned Church..........*pg. 89*

Chapter 5:
The Church Of Acts Was An Evangelistic Church.......*pg. 107*

Chapter 6:
The Church Of Acts Was An Engaged Church...........*pg. 125*

Chapter 7:
The Church Of Acts Was An Embracing Church........*pg. 141*

Chapter 8:
The Church Of Acts Was An Evolving Church...........*pg. 157*

DEDICATION

This book is dedicated to one of the greatest and wisest men I have ever known, Melvin Barnett. In my first weeks as a lead pastor, God sent a very special family to our church. They visited the Pentecostal Holiness Church on Beverly Parkway in Pensacola, Florida, in April 2001. They had two babies and almost left due to the chaos in the nursery that morning. Rev. Melvin Barnett told his wife, "I was told there is a preaching machine at this church, and I want to see if I was told right." They ended up staying and I still remember our first phone conversation. It lasted well over an hour. It seemed as if I had known Melvin my entire life.

God had not just sent me a church member and a co-laborer in the Gospel. He had sent me a friend, an encourager, and one who would provide wise counsel for the next 20 years. We became the closest of friends and worked together in some capacity for the remainder of his natural life. Brother Melvin would serve on the church council when I was under the greatest attack of my life. He defended, supported, and climbed the mountain with me in the middle of a spiritual avalanche. When the Bible talks about a friend that sticks closer than a brother, Melvin Barnett could have been in the mind of the Holy Ghost that day. I have often said that he was my Jonathan and was willing to put me ahead of himself.

Melvin became the Executive Pastor and media director of Central Chapel Pentecostal Holiness Church. While Brother Melvin served in this capacity, he created two television programs. One of those programs was *Pentecost Today*, which became the leading local Church program in Southern Alabama and Northwest Florida, reaching 1.2 million people. It was under his vision that our church services went online. Today, everyone is online. But in the early 2000s, only 3 IPH Churches (to my knowledge) could be viewed online. I can say Rev. Melvin Barnett was the most significant ally I ever had in promoting Christ and the work of

Pentecost.

Melvin Barnett was a teacher who understood the Word and knew how to expound it. Melvin Barnett was a prolific author who published the Word and spread it through print. Melvin Barnett was a producer who broadcast the Word over the airwaves. He was a trendsetter in this field. Through this media ministry, Melvin Barnett fulfilled the role of recorder. He served as a modern-day Luke: the physician archiving the movement of the Church.

Melvin Barnett was a pastor, having served several congregations. Melvin Barnett loved the people of God and cared for the flock of Christ. He was an administrator who used his gifts to advance the local church and the South Carolina Conference of the IPHC. Melvin Barnett took care of the business of God's house and made ministry more effective for those in leadership. Melvin Barnett's most significant spiritual role was that of a soul winner. I have never known a local pastor who was a more excellent soul winner - who exemplified what a Christian should be - than Melvin.

The most critical role Rev. Melvin played in my life was as a brother and friend. The night he left this world after a long cardiac battle was one of the saddest nights of my life. I cried for three days, to the point my wife thought I needed to seek counsel. His loss shook the world of all those who truly knew him. The Book of Hebrews talks about those the world was not worthy to have. I believe Melvin could fit this description as solidly as anyone I have ever known. I dedicate this book with great love and honor to my friend, a true Pentecostal leader, the Rev. Melvin Barnett.

Acts 1:1-2, "The former treatise have I made, O Theophilus, of all that Jesus began both to do and teach, Until the day in which He was taken up, after that He through the Holy Ghost had given commandments unto the apostles whom He had chosen:"

PREFACE

I am honored to write a preface to this excellent, informative book that capsulates the upstart of the early church as recorded in the Book of Acts. As you read its unfolding message, you come to realize the evolving stages the early Church engaged as the Holy Spirit brought it to its fullest impact. The dynamics expressed in these chapters were realized more so in the early days of the Pentecostal movement but regrettably have lost much of their fervor and practice in modern times.

My lifetime and personal ministry span more than 86 years. In my early years, the message of Holiness and Pentecost was the paramount subject. Regrettably, these subjects are increasingly lost to modernity, essentially replaced by seeker-friendly themes with little Biblical basis. "Old-time religion" is a relic of the past. Revival is needed. A return to Biblical teaching and preaching that sparks a hunger and thirst for the righteousness of Christ is the only answer for the church. The chapters in this book will give you fresh insights that bring resuscitation to the church that lost its breath. I highly recommend your reading of The Church on Acts.

Reverend Dr. M. Donald Duncan
Former Vice Chairman, International Pentecostal Holiness Church, Inc.

INTRODUCTION

Setting The Tone For The New Testament Church: The Church Of Acts, A Church On Fire is the sequel to *DESTINATION PENTECOST: The Baptism Of The Holy Ghost*. Our first book looked at the journey to and through Pentecost. This book will pick up where that book left off in the sense it will take us beyond the initial outpouring of the Holy Ghost and the first day of the Church. This book will give us an in-depth look at the second chapter of Acts and take us outside the Upper Room.

When Pentecostals look at Acts 2, they often have a narrow vision of this incredible chapter. If the Book of Acts were written as a book today, the first chapter would work as a preface while the second chapter would act more like the first chapter. This book will cover significant sections of the entire Book of Acts, but this writing intends to help set the tone for Acts 3-28 and into the future of Acts 29.

We are currently living in Acts 29. It has been said that the Book of Acts has no ending. This is because God intended the work of the Church and the Holy Spirit to be continual. The Book of Acts has no closing, for the Book of Acts was never meant to close. Every day we arise, we ought to be immersed in the power of the Spirit. This power is to carry out the work of the Church. It is possible we could say there was a pause to Pentecost, but there was never an end to Pentecost.

The Book of Acts is the eyewitness account of the New Testament Church as it happened. It would be the old-world equivalent of having a video camera. They had no recording devices other than parchment. Luke, the physician, took parchment in hand and recorded the testimony and his accounts, as well as the accounts of others as they occurred in real time. If the New Covenant were on trial (which it is every day), the Gospels and the Book of Acts would be the eyewitness testimony for the New Covenant. The Epistles would serve as the forensic witnesses of the New Covenant.

There is a large group of elitists in the Church that no longer care about eyewitness reports and are only concerned with the expert and forensic witnesses. The modern scholar has taken the written testimony of Paul and dismissed the eyewitness testimony. We need both solid eyewitness testimonies and the forensic testimony of the experts to make the entire case for the New Covenant. This book will aid in understanding these eyewitness reports in light of the Modern Pentecostal Church.

As the Modern Pentecostal Church searches for its place and to be accepted in today's religious landscape, it has given up much ground. It is almost as if some time back, the leaders sat down with the non-Pentecostal Church and came to a treaty. The Modern Pentecostal Church consented to quit using the gifts of the Spirit in the sanctuary and the non-Pentecostal Church would lift their hands in the sanctuary. The Modern Pentecostal church consented to quiet down and not include dancing and some extreme ways of worship in the sanctuary and the non-Pentecostal church would sing Modern Pentecostal and Charismatic songs. By the end of the treaty, the Modern Pentecostal Church and non-Pentecostal Evangelical Church would be the same. The result is that the Modern Pentecostal Church did all the giving and the non-Pentecostal Evangelical Church did all the taking. We all dropped our distinguishable names and seemingly have achieved religious unity. The question this book asks is, *"At what cost?"*

The purpose of this book is to tell the Modern Pentecostal that your foundation is the Book of Acts. The model of the Modern Pentecostal is the Church of Acts. The Church of Acts was a Church on fire and the Modern Pentecostal Church has been called to be a Church on fire. As the chorus states in the 1997 song "Church On Fire" by Russell Fragar:

This is a church on fire, this is the Holy Spirit's flame
We have a burning desire to lift Jesus name
Let the fire burn in every heart; Light the way defeat the dark
Let the flame of love burn higher
This is a church, this is a church on fire.

As a young preacher, I remember the late great preacher B. H. Clendennen saying, "Jesus is not coming back for less than He left." Jesus left a Church in waiting and He is returning for a Church in waiting. In the words of Dr. Ray H. Hughes, "Jesus left in power, Jesus is coming back in power. Jesus left in the clouds, and Jesus is coming back in the clouds. Jesus left with a body, and Jesus is coming back with a body. Jesus left the Church with a mission, and Jesus is coming back for a Church on that mission." I pray that the Modern Pentecostal Church will be that Church on mission.

John 17:18, "As thou hast sent Me into the world, even so have I also sent them into the world."

Chapter 1:

"The Modern Pentecostal Church As I See It"

Acts 20:28, *"Take heed therefore unto yourselves, and to all the flock, over the which the Holy Ghost hath made you overseers, to **feed the Church of God**, which He hath purchased with His Own blood."*

I was born and raised in the Church of God, headquartered in Cleveland, Tennessee. I used to say, "I am Church of God born, Church of God bred, and when I die, I will be Church of God dead." When I say I loved the Church of God, it was more than an expression. To be honest, it was almost like an addiction. Even my clothes had the Church of God symbol on them. For Christmas one year, my best friend, Dr. Jerry Jeter, who had started in the ministry a year after I did, went to the mall and had red sweatshirts made for our mothers with the words "Church Of God Preacher's Mom" embroidered on the front of them.

All my heroes were Church of God preachers

with some AG preachers like Pastor Glyn Lowery and Evangelist Jimmy Swaggart getting in there. I loved Dr. Ray H. Hughes. He might as well have been the 4th member of the Trinity as far as I was concerned. There has never been a rock star who could reach the sounds of a man like John D. Nichols, who was my dad's favorite preacher. I know most people reading this book will have never heard of most of these men, but these were the men who built me, the men I wanted to be. In my eyes, these were men larger than life. As I said, they were my heroes. No organization could make heroes like the Church of God. The authority with which these men carried themselves was awe-inspiring for a teenage preacher boy.

The first time I ever flew was when I was 17 years old. I flew from Pensacola, Florida, to San Antonio, Texas, for the 1990 Church of God General Assembly. I had saved my own money to purchase my airfare and lodging for that week. I will never forget boarding the plane with a King James Bible in one hand and a copy of "Like A Mighty Army" (The History of the Church of God) in the other hand. I was off on the adventure of my life. I can still remember the feeling of being in that giant auditorium with thousands of other Church of God people. I got to meet Dr. Wade H. Horton on the streets of San Antonio that week. I might as well have met the Apostle Paul. I could not have been more excited to meet anyone unless it had been Dr. Ray H. Hughes.

In 1992, Jerry Jeter, (my best friend who was more like a brother) and I went in with a Church of God preacher out of Crestview, Florida, and rented a cabin at the Church of God Campground in Wimauma, Florida. It was exciting to be on that old historic campground. All the streets were named after great Church of God preachers, and we were staying on the road named for Rev. James Cross. The preacher who was renting the cabin with us was also a podiatrist. One morning, Jerry and I decided to sleep in and not go to morning Bible study. He was lying in his little room on one side of the hall and I was in my little room on the other. It must have hit us simultaneously. We met in the hall and with shocked faces, said, "Is it him?" Dr. Ray H. Hughes was sitting in the kitchen of our little cabin with his shoes off and feet up in Dr. Elis's lap as Dr. Elis was working on his feet. We were so embarrassed we had not gone to morning service, but neither of us could pass up the opportunity to meet Dr. Ray H. Hughes. Sometimes, you get to meet your heroes, but you cannot choose where you meet them.

The Pentecostal Church is extensive and consists of more organizations than any other church movement, but I want to share my perspective as we talk about the Modern Pentecostal church. My perspective is just one, but I now classify myself as a hybrid Pentecostal. I was raised in the Church of God, started ministry in the Church of God, and evangelized in the Church of God. The Church of God of the 1990's has been and still is the greatest spiritual influence on my life. Even with the great influence of the Church of God, my understanding of the Modern Pentecostal Church goes beyond the Church of God. I was privileged to attend four different Christian Schools from K5 to 12th grade.

The last school I attended in my early education was operated by a Oneness Pentecostal Apostolic church named *Spoken Word*. This was one of the greatest moves of my life. Though I adamantly disagree with much of the Oneness Pentecostal doctrine, this experience gave me a broader understanding of the Pentecostal Church. It gave me a drive to learn more about my own spiritual heritage. If I had not attended Spoken Word, I would have never searched the Scriptures and had the interest in the Pentecostal Movement I now have. Though I disagree with much of their thinking, much of it challenges me to be both a better person and a better Pentecostal. I can say I am who I am because of what they either taught me or challenged me to become.

After four years of traveling the southeastern United States as a full-time evangelist, I was tired. Even at the very young age of 27, I was getting worn out. I would preach seven times a week and spend all day Saturday traveling to my next destination. I did not know how to book a revival back in those days and I would close out a revival on Friday night in North Tennessee and start a revival the following Sunday in South Florida. I just put people wherever they wanted to be. I would typically book 9 to 10 weeks at a time, come home, do tree work with my dad for a week or two, and hit the road again. In 1997, I preached five and a half months straight with no real break. I ended up getting sick after that long stint of revivals but continued to go without stopping.

One of the greatest revivals I ever preached was at a church in the Chattanooga area called Red Bank Church of God. We had a powerful time! The church was full every night and the power of God was on display. On the last night of the revival, a Friday night, the pastor looked over at me and said, "The biggest crowd we ever had in this church was 286, and that was this past Easter." He said, "There are more here tonight than we had for Easter." The pastor asked me to stay on, but I kept such a strict schedule that I told him I needed to go. I left that awesome atmosphere to drive to Jacksonville, Florida, to start a revival that never had more than 40 to 50 people any given night.

In that revival at the Otis Road Church of God, I learned the most valuable lesson I would learn in ministry. Remember, revivals and church in general are not all about crowds but what you leave and what you take away. It was my habit even - after having come off long nights of revival and driving hundreds and hundreds of miles - to preach every Sunday morning, work the altars, and then go to lunch with the pastor. I would always go back to the church and pray and study for the evening service right up to the evening service. Pastor Doyle Williams looked at me and could see how exhausted I was. This wise older pastor said these words and they forever changed my life. "Brother Tim, sometimes the most spiritual thing you can do is rest when you are tired." Those words had a profound effect on my life, and I started resting every Sunday afternoon. I learned that God continued to move even though I was resting because the service depended on Him, not me.

After these fantastic years as a Church of God

evangelist, a true dream of mine came true: to preach at the Pace Assembly of God Church in Pace, Florida, under the leadership of Rev. Glyn Lowery. Pace was the Pentecostal powerhouse within three states. In so many ways, it was the gold standard of a large Pentecostal church. I could have only dreamed of ever preaching in this great church. I still remember being so nervous to preach on that Sunday night. It was my first time feeling genuinely nervous about preaching in years. It was an excellent service, and they asked me to return very soon. Eventually, I went on staff at Pace Assembly and came off the road. I was there for 14 long months. I knew when I went off the road, I was out of the will of God. I even told the Lord, "I don't think this is your will, but will You please let me do it anyway?" Like Israel, who wanted a king when God was pleased to be their King, God gave in to my request. And like Israel, God allowing me to do this was not without repercussions.

This is in no way any reflection of Pace Assembly or Rev Glyn Lowery. I love both the church and the man greatly to this day. No, it reflects a child preacher who wanted it his way. This decision to step out of God's will led me down a road of other bad choices, negatively affecting my life forever. I ended up leaving the Church of God and joined the International Pentecostal Holiness Church. I went to pastor the IPH Church in Pensacola and this church would be the vehicle for my future. The church in Pensacola helped me survive and stood by me through the most challenging time of my life. After seven years of pastoring and having started a successful radio and television program, the time came for me to leave my hometown.

I had preached a revival at the Mt Beulah Pentecostal Holiness for one of the dearest friends God would ever give me, Rev Melvin Barnett. While in revival at that church, I felt God calling me to pastor in Lake City, SC. I told Brother Melvin that I thought God was calling me to Lake City. I then told him they would not want me. I am not from SC, and I am single. I told my friend I would not want a single pastor. Brother Melvin said these words that changed my life, "You let them make that decision. You don't make that decision for them." I returned to Pensacola and called the Bishop. He set up an interview and trial sermon. I can still remember driving up I-95 and passing the SC State line. As soon as I passed the line, I heard the Holy Spirit say, "You are home."

I pulled up in front of a large, beautiful home and was greeted by a wonderful older gentleman named Randy Teal (a year and a half later, Randy Teal would become my grandfather-in-law). Brother Teal took me to see the church. I already knew this was where God had called me without ever being in a service and having no facts about the church. That evening, I met with the Church Council and answered all their questions. The following day, I preached in the worship service, and by that afternoon, I was officially the lead pastor of the Lake City Pentecostal Holiness Church. It was a good thing because I had already resigned from my church, rented my house out, and sold all my furniture. If the Lake City Pentecostal Holiness Church had rejected me, I would have been churchless, jobless, and homeless.

At the time of this writing, I have been Lead Pastor of this great church for nearly 16 years. Only God knows how appreciative I am to be the Lead Pastor of the Lake City Pentecostal Holiness Church. I met my wife soon after I arrived in Lake City. She was a 4th generation in the Lake City PH Church. Our children would be the first 5th generation born into the Lake City Pentecostal Holiness Church.

Though Lake City was a nearly 75 year old classical Pentecostal Church, it was a culture shock for me. Lake City PH was a much more liberal church in terms of dress than I had ever worked with. At that time, dress was a big thing for me and had been since I was a young teenager. They were also not nearly as demonstrative of a church as the Pensacola Pentecostal Holiness church. There were times I thought I had made a mistake in coming, but I knew God had called me to this church. Over the years, they became more conservative in their dress, and I became more liberal on the subject. I can say we met in the middle on these nonessential issues. I would also say that Lake City

Pentecostal Holiness Church is now among the most demonstrative Pentecostal churches in South Carolina. It was a great church from day one; we were just very different. Lake City PH and I grew together and they have provided me with a loving church family and taken care of me and my family as well as any church could take care of a pastor. I say again, it is my great privilege to pastor this great church and to help pastor the town of Lake City, SC.

I have taken this time to give you my personal ministry journey and an idea of where I am coming from concerning the Modern Pentecostal Church. I am old enough to remember when the Pentecostal church made significant transitions. I remember the first time I saw a woman wear pants to church. I remember when we went from singing hymns and convention songs with a call-up choir with a piano to singing modern choruses with a full band. Things like ear piercings and pants, especially among ministry families, were a big deal when I was born. Today, these things are nonissues in most churches. Several years ago, my wife and I attended a gathering of Pentecostal church leaders from several Pentecostal organizations. We walked into the Northwood Temple sanctuary, the 2,500-seat auditorium of one of the largest IPHC congregations in the United States. To our surprise, every woman in that church was wearing pants. This is only to point out that this issue went from very important to non-existent.

The Modern Pentecostal Church has made several moves over the years away from some of its early teachings. Some of these things were just cultural and we must recognize that culture has its place. This did not make our forefathers wrong or ignorant. They were simply living the culture both inside and outside of the Church of that day. I call these things "furniture". Every generation has the right to change the furniture in their house. You do not have to keep Grandma's style to serve Grandma's God. No generation has the right to touch the foundation and structure of this Spiritual house.

For every generation, the house/Church has a

foundation. The foundation of the Church is the Blood of Jesus. The Church is built on the life, death, resurrection, return, and reign of Jesus Christ. No group has the right to change the foundation of the House. The load-bearing walls of this house, called the Church, are sanctification and holiness. It is sanctification and holiness that protect from the winds of worldliness. The roof or covering of this house is the power of the Holy Ghost. It is the Holy Ghost's power that pulls the Church together. Under the power of the Holy Ghost, every joint is fitly put together and supplied for. This house is the Church as long as it is founded upon Christ, surrounded by the Word, and covered by the Spirit. If you remove the Word or the Spirit or tweak the foundation by adding to or diluting from, this structure is no longer the Church, and it becomes altogether something different.

I want to be perfectly clear on this point: I am not fighting for tradition. No daughter-in-law should keep her mother-in-law's couch. I am fighting to keep the structure of the Church. Wear what you feel good about wearing. Take off your wingtips and put on tennis shoes. Take off your tie and untuck your shirt. None of these things matter to me. I am still going to dress like I like to dress and what I feel is pleasing to God. I expect you to dress how you feel is pleasing to God. If you do not feel any way about that, don't worry about it. As the Apostle said, "But if any man seems to be contentious, we have no such custom, neither the churches of God."

The Modern Pentecostal Church can be modern and still be Pentecostal. I am not so concerned about what you wear when you are preaching as I am what you are preaching. Young men and young women, be your authentic selves. Do not be trapped in any other person's style and do not reject tradition for rejection's sake. Be open enough to the Holy Ghost to allow Him to mold you and make you into what He wants you to be. Young men and young women, if you want to be Pentecostal, you must preach the atoning blood of Jesus. You must preach the resurrection, return, and reign of Christ. Young men and young women, preach holiness, preach separation from the worldview that forgets God has an unchangeable standard. Hear the admonition from Paul to his spiritual son, "Preach the Word; be instant in season, out of season; reprove, rebuke, exhort with all long suffering and Doctrine." Man and woman of God, preach the Holy Ghost and preach with the Holy Ghost. Do not be ashamed of His power and do not be afraid of His power.

The Modern Pentecostal Church has every right to be modern. The Modern Pentecostal Church does not have the right to take away the Pentecostal part. If you are reading this book and you reject Pentecostalism, please do not stay in the Pentecostal movement. There are plenty of wonderful Evangelical churches that could use you. If you question everything you were ever taught, get on your knees and in your Word until you reconcile these things in your heart. If you are part of a Pentecostal organization and you still believe our Church's cardinal doctrines, we need you.

The Modern Pentecostal Movement needs us to preach the Word. Create an atmosphere that is about

God and God will be there. Create an atmosphere that is about people and people will be there. Here is the biggest issue I see in the Modern Pentecostal Church: we do not know how to do both and we have settled with one or the other. We must create an atmosphere through our worship and the Word that builds a habitation for the Holy Ghost to dwell in. Explain to the people what is happening, but do not dismiss the Holy Spirit in order to entertain the flesh. Find out what grieves the Holy Spirit and do the opposite. If the Spirit of God is in control and if He is made welcome, He will perform His good Word and work toward us. He will draw people to Himself and bring about true conversion.

John 12:32, "And I, if I be lifted up from the earth, will draw all men unto Me."

This is not a choice of God over man. This is a choice of God over everything. This is trusting God enough to have His way in your services. People can get out of line. I understand and have had to deal with it. Let us not throw the baby out with the bathwater. Let us not throw sincere saints trying to be obedient to God out with some bad actors. The Modern Pentecostal Church, in an attempt to correct the craziness of the past, has over-corrected. We have gone from carnal craziness to religious ritual and forgotten the place of the Holy Spirit in our services. People should know they are in a Pentecostal Church - even in a Modern Pentecostal Church.

Matthew 16:18, "And I say also unto thee, That thou art Peter, and upon this rock I will build My Church; and the Gates of Hell shall not prevail against it."

Chapter 2:

"Peter's Message At Pentecost"

Acts 2:22-26, "Ye men of Israel, hear these words; Jesus of Nazareth, a man approved of God among you by miracles and wonders and signs, which God did by Him in the midst of you, as ye yourselves also know: Him, being delivered by the determinate counsel and foreknowledge of God, ye have taken, and by wicked hands have crucified and slain: Whom God hath raised up, having loosed the pains of death: because it was not possible that He should be holden of it. For David speaketh concerning Him, I foresaw the Lord always before my face, for He is on my right hand, that I should not be moved: Therefore did my heart rejoice, and my tongue was glad; moreover, also my flesh shall rest in hope:"

As a lifelong Pentecostal, the second chapter of Acts was as prominent as John 3:16. Many of the messages I would hear preached growing up came from Acts 2. campmeeting preachers started many of their messages from Acts 2. The vast majority of those messages were from the first four verses. I recall Rod Parsley being the first I heard say, "Turn your Bibles to Pentecostal Headquarters", though I have said it 100 times since then. This was referring to Acts 2:1-4. Acts 2:1-4 has always been an important part of my life. When my children were small, I taught them to quote it along with John 3:16 and the Lord's Prayer.

In the 9th grade, I started attending Spoken Word Christian School. Spoken Word was an Apostolic Oneness Church and I attended their services almost as much as I did my own church. I went to every revival, which they had several times a year. I went as often as my parents would allow me to go. I loved that church. I loved the way they worshipped. I loved the way they got in the altar. They also introduced me to a new part of Acts chapter 2 which, of course, was verse 38. I just thought we liked Acts 2:1-4, but Acts 2:1-4 did not hold a candle to how much they loved Acts 2:38. I cannot recall one message preached by one Apostolic preacher that did not reference Acts 2:38. I know the Bible is the

Word of God. Still, if it is possible to worship a single verse of Scripture, they accomplished it.

When I started preaching, my favorite living preacher was Ray H. Hughes. He is now my favorite preacher of the past. Dr. Hughes could not only preach Acts 2:1-4, but also Acts 2:14-21. I loved listening to him quote those verses and then break them down. Over the years, I have also grabbed hold of these passages and exegete them. In the following chapters of this book, we will do just that and look at these powerful verses from Acts and reference back to Joel. I will not do the job of Ray H. Hughes, but by the power of the Spirit, we will see these powerful verses come to life.

In my own preaching, the Book of Acts has been a staple. My wife has often said if it were not for the Book of Acts, I would have nothing to preach. Her closest friend told her one day, "I have never heard Tim preach that he did not preach out of Acts chapter 2." I suppose I am guilty of preaching from this passage as much as any preacher I know. It was what was preached to me, and I love preaching it. When I wrote my first book, the subject was to no one's surprise. When I announced I was writing this book, it was assumed it would be on the Holy Ghost and deal with Acts 2:1-4.

Several years ago, I was looking at Acts 2 and reading over the highlights. I was hearing the wind and feeling the fire. I listened to them speak with other tongues as the Spirit gave them the utterance. I walked with them out of the Upper Room onto the streets of Jerusalem and heard them preach the wonderful works of God in known languages. I watched the amazement on the faces of all learned people as these poor fishermen spoke in their perfect tongues. Then I saw Peter stand up with the eleven, lift up his voice, and quote from that Old Testament prophet we all love so much by the name of Joel. After experiencing this again for the hundredth time, I jumped over to verses 37 – 44 and saw the explosive continual growth of the Church. As I made this all too familiar journey over this inaugural day of celebration, I realized that I must have stepped out to the foyer during the sermon.

All my adult life, I have noted that preachers can often be like children. My children get so hungry and thirsty when it is time for the preaching to start. My poor children, along with many other children, have a host of issues that require them to step out of church at the start of preaching. It is not just children. In the South, many southern mamas and good Christian southern grandmothers sacrifice the preaching every Sunday morning so they can go home and get lunch on the table. Heaven forbid if they stayed in the service and actually listened to the preaching! Help us, Lord, if Junior and Grand Junior did not have their lunch on the table as soon as church was over! After all, that was the main reason they came to church in the first place. There are some excellent Christians I would question if they were ever actually present for the entire sermon.

There is always that group of "holier than thou" preachers who camp outside during campmeeting. Some sit out during the music because it is too contemporary for their liking. This gives them a chance to gather with all their friends and discuss how poorly things are being run and how much better they could do. Then we have preachers who like the music, but don't care for the preacher. Then, some really came to campmeeting just for fellowship. Sadly, some preachers only come to church when they are on the program or getting paid. This must have been what had happened to me in Acts 2. I got there for worship, was there during the shouting time, and returned to the altar, but missed the message.

All these years as a Pentecostal, all the campmeetings and revivals, I could not recall anyone preaching Peter's message that day. I heard the opening of Peter's message. I heard that this is that part of the message. These are the good quotations that got the church to shout. Somehow, I missed the meat of the message. On this day, as I surveyed Acts 2, I got to thinking I missed the message. The message has to be important because of three things. First, the *reason for* the message. Secondly, the *response to* the message. Thirdly, the *results of* the message. I believe this message was worth listening to. This message is worth missing the foyer fellowship. This message was worth forgoing the denominational gospel gossip. This message was worth staying to hear what God had to say to His Church. The next time we are at campmeeting, let us think about how important it is to listen to what God has to say.

Peter had a *reason for* preaching this message. This message would be God's inaugural address to the world concerning His Church. When a man or woman of God stands under the anointing of God and preaches the Word of God being led by the Spirit of God, they are speaking for God. In all actuality, Peter was speaking for God on this day. These were not the ramblings of an uneducated fisherman. This was the oracle of Heaven speaking on behalf of God. Peter preaches this message to give God a voice. B. H. Clendennen used to say, "We are simply containers for God to live in." Through us, God rides in cars and travels the roads of life. Through us, God stays in hotels and stands in the lobby. Through us, God maneuvers in this world. This is only made possible when we become containers of the presence and life of God. We become containers of His presence and life when we are filled with His Holy Spirit. Peter was such a container. When Peter preached, he preached for God. Peter became like the Old Testament Prophet Jeremiah. It was like a fire shut up in his bones.

The reason Peter preached this first message on the Day of Pentecost was that he was giving God a voice. The voice of God was speaking prophetically through the preacher. The connection between anointed Holy Ghost preaching and prophecy cannot be severed. As a matter of fact, prophecy is what true Holy Ghost anointed preaching is. We think the difference between preaching and teaching is speed and volume. We measure anointed preaching by sweat. Teaching is explaining the works of God. Preaching is displaying the works of God. When I teach, I explain God's Word. But, when I preach, I proclaim God's Word. The Holy Ghost preaches through human assistance. Preaching speaks for God. This is why none of us should miss what the preacher is saying. It is more important than your

Sunday afternoon lunch. It is more important than the fellowship meeting taking place in the parking lot. We might get more done if we listen to God through the preacher. I have heard it said there has been enough preaching to save ten worlds. To that, I say we have not even saved one yet.

What was the reason for Peter's message? God preached the message, with Peter being His mouthpiece, to establish the central theme of the Church. The theme of the Church is Jesus of Nazareth, a man approved by God. The entire message is about Jesus, and the entire Church is about Jesus. Jesus should be the central theme for all our messages. The reason Peter preached was to point people to Jesus. The reason we preach is to point people to Jesus. From out of Jesus flows all God has for us. Jesus is the Rock from which the living water flows. Jesus is the Word made flesh. As one Church of God preacher said, "Good preaching is telling Bible stories and bragging about Jesus." This is really what this first Pentecostal message did. It told the critical truth of the Bible and revealed Jesus.

Peter preached many great messages. The two that stand out in Acts would be his first message here in Acts 2 and the message he preached in Acts 10. The message in Acts 2 connected the Jews to Jesus. This message gave the Church thrust and aligned the Jews with Jesus. The message in Acts 10 connected the Gentiles with Jesus. It brought forth the power of the Holy Ghost and grafted the Gentile bride into the Church. Both messages were intended to bring thrust and connect people to Jesus. It is important that we, as preachers, ask, "Does our preaching bring thrust and does it connect people to Jesus?" If your preaching - both the preaching you do and the preaching you hear - is not doing these two things, it has lost its reason for preaching. God places a lot of stock in reason and purpose. God has a purpose for all He does and desires us to operate in purpose.

The second thing to look at concerning Peter's message was the *response to* the message. Peter preaches this message to lift Jesus and tell the Jews that Jesus is their Messiah. The response to this message was incredible. Three thousand souls were added to the Church that day. I have spent most of my life as an evangelist. I have preached for souls. When I first started preaching in our little Church of God with about 60 people in attendance, I preached on Sunday nights and we called that our "evangelistic service". It did not matter if there were only 30 people and I knew everyone. It did not matter if all had been at the altar that morning crying out to God and speaking in tongues. It did not matter if they were all the solid workers in the church. I was going to give an altar call. One of the men said to the pastor, "We need to get some sinners in the church, so Brother Tim can have someone to invite to the altar." Most preachers preach for a response.

I have often said that I am a response-driven preacher. It does affect me when people do not respond. They do not have to be shouting or running the pews, but give me some sign you are listening. Taking notes is nice. It may be their grocery list or doodling but, as far as I know, they write every word I say. If you are not a note-taker, you could be a "nodder." Just nod your head in agreement. That is good. I know you are hearing me. If you do not like to clap, say "Amen!" or "Preach!", and if you do not like to take notes and nod, smile. Smiling would be a definite improvement over a frown or a blank expression. I would almost rather have the congregation mad than non-responsive.

So many churches are non-responsive. If you were to go into your grandmother's house and find her on the floor, the first thing you would do is speak to her. If she did not talk back, you would get on the ground with her and nudge her to see if she was asleep. If after you did everything you could do to get her to speak and she did not respond, you would call for medical help. Once the paramedics came, they would check out her vitals and determine her life force. They would then carry her to the hospital if she had no response. The last thing you would do is say, "Well, she is not dead. Maybe she will wake up tomorrow." The fact she still had a pulse would not cut it.

Nonresponsive is not an acceptable state

for a living person. Yet we have thousands of Pentecostal churches that are non-responsive, and because they still have a pulse, we consider this an acceptable state. Response matters. It matters if the church responds. Though we as preachers should not solely preach for a response, response matters. Just like you would not leave your nonresponsive grandmother on the floor, we cannot leave our nonresponsive church members in the pew. When a man or woman of God is preaching God's Word, they speak for God. When God is speaking, we should be at attention. When God asks a question, we should answer. We should spiritually evaluate our lives and respond appropriately when altar calls are given. Life should rise up in us at the sound of His name and voice.

Preacher, if you provide altar call after altar call, week after week, and there is no response, something is wrong. How do you check the life of a Pentecostal church? Look at the altar and see what kind of use they have. If the altars are not used, you do not have a sanctuary; you have a lecture hall. I don't look to fill the altar when I teach, but I am preaching for a response when I preach. That altar determines the immediate strength of that message.

The response to Peter's message was phenomenal. We see a response by them asking a question. The message has concluded, and at the end of this message, this Jewish audience has been moved. They have moved past all they have ever been taught. They have moved past all of Jesus' bad press. They ask the question, what must we do? This response from Peter caused him to instruct them on what a Christian looks like. They hear the instructions and respond in obedience. It was not a simple "bow your head, close your eyes, and slip up your hand". Peter says if you are serious, get out of the sinning business. If you want to be a Christian, follow Christ in death and resurrection by being water-baptized. If you want Jesus right now, start seeking the baptism of the Holy Ghost.

This reminds me of our old Pentecostals who, as soon as someone had prayed through to salvation, wanted them to get sanctified. They wanted them to be baptized in the Holy Ghost as soon as they could testify of God's sanctifying power in their lives. This kind of requirement of response is what fueled the New Testament Church and propelled the early Pentecostal Church from a handful of members to hundreds and hundreds of millions of Pentecostal believers. This response caused 3,000 people to bow before God and make Jesus their Lord and Savior that day.

This message Peter preached that day cannot be ignored because he preached it. This message Peter preached that day cannot be overlooked due to the response he got from preaching it. This message Peter preached that day cannot be ignored due to the result of preaching it. Some messages are preached for the right reason and even produce a response, but they have no long-lasting results. The response is awesome, but the result is eternal. The response is fleeting and temporal. They responded to Jesus riding in on a colt with words of adoration and praise. They were caught up in the moment. But, when the moment changed, the song changed. They went from chanting "Blessed be the King!" to "Crucify Him!" all on a whim.

I have found this to be the case in so many of our modern altar calls. I used to see the response from the Sunday services on Facebook every Sunday and Monday. They would post five saved, ten saved, and so forth. At the rate they saw people saved, they should have outgrown their facilities in a few months. Street evangelists often love to tout all the salvation they have seen in a town or a community. I remember one of the last years I was in the Church of God, they put out a report of the people saved in Church of God altars that year and it was not far from their total membership.

What I am saying is the response and results are not the same—most of what we count as results is seed casting. We are doing right by casting seeds. We are doing right by praying with people. We are doing right by getting out of the four walls of our churches and reaching the lost. Where we are going wrong is thinking responses are equivalent to results.

The response is temporal. It makes you feel good and it makes the one responding feel good. Response is easy and often gets people off your back. When I ask my children to do something, they often respond with "Yes, I will." The problem is this response is often empty and produces no result. If I ask my baby daughter to feed and water the dogs and she says "yes", she has responded. If she goes to bed without feeding and watering the dogs, the dogs go lacking. If this happens enough, they will die. If I asked my daughter something that required a response and she did not respond, action would be taken. Her response is not equal to her obedience. When there is no response, something is wrong, but the response is not equal to obedience. For too long, the Church has rested on its ability to get people to respond while the children are dying in their sins and trespasses. The goal is not to get people to respond or get them to the altar. The goal is to get people to Heaven - and that only comes by spiritual results.

The message Peter preached at Pentecost produced eternal results. It was this message that hit the mark of reason. This message was preached for the right reason. The message Peter preached hit the mark of response. Three thousand responded to the invitation.

Most importantly, it's the mark of results, for this message steadied the Church and left a group of devoted Jesus followers who made the name of Jesus famous everywhere they went. These souls were sold out and they became part of the Church. Notice they joined themselves to the Church. Results do not just make people "Christians." Results make people followers of Jesus. Followers of Jesus follow Jesus by becoming faithful to His Church. Going to church will not make you a Christian, no more than sleeping in a garage will make you a car. If you are a Christian, you realize the way the Kingdom is advanced is through the health of the Church and you will do all you can to make sure the Church is as healthy, stable, and strong as it possibly can be.

What was the result of Peter's message at Pentecost? There is a Church today. Peter's message at

Pentecost deserves the time and effort for it to be heard. May all our messages be so powerful they meet the level of God's reason for preaching. May all our messages move the hearer to respond. May all our messages produce lasting and eternal results as the message Peter preached on that day. How appropriate that Peter - the first person to ever declare that Jesus is divine - would preach this first message on the Day of Pentecost! May we, as the Pentecostal Movement, apologize to Peter for focusing all our attention on the opening of Acts 2 and the closing of Acts 2 while ignoring the heart of Acts 2.

As we watch the service from that day, let us not do like many people do today and fast forward past the parts we do not like or the parts we do not think are interesting. The writing of this book is about getting to Acts 2 early before the service starts and staying to the last amen. We want to watch the announcements on the screen, listen to the opening prayer, and wait for every part of the service including the message. In fact, I want it to be like it was when I was growing up: let the pastor lock up the church while we sat in the parking lot talking after church. We desire to squeeze and siege every moment of this day of Pentecost and all the events of Acts chapter 2.

Luke 22:31-32, "And the Lord said, Simon, Simon, behold, Satan hath desired to have you, that he may sift you as wheat: But I have prayed for thee, that thy faith fail not: and when thou art converted, strengthen thy brethren."

Chapter 3:

"The Church Of Acts Was An Empowered Church"

Acts 2:1-4, "And when the day of Pentecost was fully come, they were all with one accord in one place. And suddenly there came a sound from heaven as of a rushing mighty wind, and it filled all the house where they were sitting. And there appeared unto them cloven tongues like as of fire, and it sat upon each of them. And they were all filled with the Holy Ghost, and began to speak with other tongues, as the Spirit gave them utterance."

Right out of the gate, we look at the first four verses of Acts 2 and are introduced to the first characteristic of the New Testament Church—the first in respect to time and placement, not the first in respect to importance. Sometimes, because something comes first, we think that makes it the most important. Ask any eldest child, and they will say this is the case. Sometimes, the first is not the most important, but simply what they got first. Ask any youngest child and they will tell you, "They finally got it right, so they stopped." As we move forward, I want to establish there are times when what is listed first is chief, but this is not one of those times.

Since we spent almost an entire book looking at what happened before Acts chapter 2, we will not spend much time there. I do think it is important to understand the Church was in waiting prior to Acts 2:2. Waiting speaks to our priorities. Waiting speaks to our patience. Waiting speaks to our pain. The fact the Church was willing to wait these 7 to 10 days tells where they were spiritually. They would have had to adjust their schedules to be there. They would have had to miss work and money. They would have had to sleep on a hard floor. They had no Uber Eats, so they were missing meals. Every comfort was suspended in order for them to wait.

When was the last time you were so desperate to receive something you were willing to suspend every comfort to get it? Children do it for movies and concerts. They will wait in line all night to pay an astronomical price to hear someone sing. People wait for technology. They will camp outside a store for the latest phone or device and then pay a thousand dollars. Parents will sit in blazing heat and blistering cold to watch their kids play a game. There is a lot that can be said about waiting. There is a lot that can be said about your unwillingness to wait. Remember, five hundred received the command to wait, but only 120 waited. Have you ever been so excited about anything to do with God that you were willing to wait?

In 1998, the most prominent Pentecostal preacher in America had to be Pastor Rod Parsley. I can still remember the Sunday afternoon in 1994 when I saw Rod Parsley on television for the first time. It had not been since Jimmy Swaggart that I had watched a preacher on TV who had impressed me more than Rod Parsley. I wanted to be just like him. He was everything I thought I wanted to be. So when he was booked to preach the Sunday afternoon service at the Florida

Church of God Campmeeting, it was the greatest thing in my life coming together. I loved the Florida State Campmeeting more than any other event in the year. I loved Rod Parsley more than any other preacher in America. For Rod Parsley to preach at the Wimauma Campmeeting was as close to Heaven as anything would get on this earth to this young Church of God evangelist. I had to preach that morning for about an hour at the Land O' Lakes Church of God. I can't remember anything about that service. All I had on my mind was getting back to the campground.

The tabernacle at Wimauma would seat 5,200 people with the choir and they put out hundreds and hundreds of extra seats. It did not matter. I had to be there and I had to have as close a seat to the action as I could. I passed every restaurant to get back to Wimauma. I got there and I waited. And I waited. And I waited, and I waited, and I waited. Hours and hours passed as I sat on those very uncomfortable tabernacle chairs. The longer I waited, the more uncomfortable they became. Finally, the service began and, in Church of God fashion, we spent time. We sang, and we sang, and we used every good singer we had. The offering, of course, was a big deal. We could not just pass the plate. A compelling Biblical case had to be made about why we must give our biggest offering. The Bishop's family joined him for this event and they - along with every other important person in the room of several thousand people - had to be recognized. By the time Rod Parsley got up to preach, all I wanted was for the service to end. I told my friend who had waited with me, "Only if Jesus in the flesh comes will I ever wait this long to hear someone preach again."

The Church waited. They did not just wait an hour or a day, but for over a week, they waited. They had no climate-controlled building to wait in. They had no padded seats to sit in. They had no modern amenities to assist them in their wait. If they had had them, they might not have waited. They had a burning desire to see whatever this promise was that Jesus was sending to them. Most could not hang, but there were 120 who were willing to die in that upper chamber. They were not going anywhere. They had already decided what Jesus had promised was worth the wait. Until this Church age concludes that what Jesus has for them is worth the wait and cost, they will not walk in what He intended them to walk in. I ask you right now to determine in your heart that whatever God has for you is worth the wait. Rod Parsley may not be worth the wait. That concert or that iPhone may not be worth the wait. I assure you what God has promised is worth the wait.

Suddenly, the power and the promise came. As one preacher said, "God may not come quickly, but He always comes suddenly." By Day 7 or Day 10, they had probably established a pattern to their waiting. I would have, as well. They must have wondered if they had got what they were looking for. Have you ever been waiting for something, but you did not quite know what you were waiting for? Maybe someone started moaning and they thought, "Is this it?" Maybe someone started crying and thought, "Is this it?" On and on, we could go with human emotion with which they could have misread the room. Suddenly, He came - and when He came, there was no doubt it was Him. I want to tell you that when the real Holy Ghost comes, there is no doubt it is Him. The Holy Ghost always takes over the room. He certainly took over the room that day. The Upper Room became His room and He filled every part of it. He filled the room where they were sitting, and the sounds, sights, and sensations of Pentecost were on display.

Think about the sound of that rushing, mighty wind. One version of the Bible called it a mighty tempest blast. This was not the sound of a breeze on a hot day. This was not even the sound of a howling wind on a cold night. No, what you need to think about is hurricane-force winds and the sound of a tornado. The sound of a locomotive running through that upper room. A lady told me one day, "Pentecostals think loud is good, and louder is better." To that, I replied, "We serve a loud God." When God walks in the room, He stomps in the room. When God came down on Mount Sinai, He came down with thunder and required the trumpets to blow loudly. They blew so loud and so much noise was made that the dirt under their feet began to reverberate. I can't find where the Bible ever commands us to praise God quietly. I know God is not deaf, but He is also not nervous. It was with a great sound He entered, and it should be with a great sound we should make it known He is in the room.

They were in an upper chamber
They were all in one accord,
When the Holy Ghost descended
As was promised by the Lord.
O Lord, send the pow'r just now,
O Lord, send the pow'r just now,
O Lord, send the pow'r just now and baptize ev'ry one.

"O Lord, Send The Power Just Now"
Charles D. Tillman (1895)

Let the Holy Ghost from Heaven fall on me!
Let the Holy Ghost from Heaven fall on me!
I will sing about Him, shout about Him,
talk about Him to everyone I meet,
Let the Holy Ghost from Heaven fall on me.

"Let The Holy Ghost From Heaven Fall On Me"
Bill Waters (Church of God Publishing)

Send it on down, send it on down,
Lord, let the Holy Ghost come on down.
Heavenly Father, hear our call,
Let Your Holy Spirit fall,
Send down the power, let it fall like rain,
As we lift our praises to Your name.

"Send It On Down"
Geron Davis (1994; DaviShop Publishing)

These are some of the lyrics that have fueled Pentecostal services. They are the request of the Holy Ghost to come. Those in the Upper Room would not have known to ask for these things, but I feel assured they were praying, singing, and petitioning in whatever way they could for the Holy Ghost to come. I wonder how many of the songs we sing today are making requests for the Spirit to fall. Even more important than our songs, how many of our messages focus people on His power? The real question is, how many of our altar calls are invitations for the Holy Ghost to fill our lives? We place focus on what we prioritize. I have seen very little focus in our singing, preaching, or altar calls on the Baptism of the Holy Ghost. This Pentecostal Church was born in fire.

Years ago, I was at a community service in Lake City. The churches represented at the service were Baptist, Methodist, Presbyterian, and Pentecostal. All these pastors are dear friends of mine. The Methodist pastor preached a message from Ezekiel chapter 37 dealing with the valley of the dead, dry bones. I told my friend that the Methodist pastor had preached from a Pentecostal passage. There was no true Pentecostal preacher worth their salt that did not have at least one message from this passage. My good friend, who is the pastor of First Baptist, said, "Well, I guess we know now that Ezekiel was a Pentecostal." I replied, "All the writers of the New Testament were Pentecostal." Pastor Shane said, "Now, you have to give us John the Baptist." I said, "Sorry, Pastor Shane. John was filled with the Holy Ghost from the womb and was the first to preach the Baptism of the Holy Ghost, so I cannot give you that one."

It was a regular day and the Pharisee class came out to see why things were so quiet on the streets and in the marketplace. It was reported to them that the town had emptied to hear that wild-eyed evangelist prophet by the name of John. This group of religious leaders decided to see what all the fuss was about. When John saw them coming, he put the bad mouth on them. He called them vile names and told them they were full of foolish pride. He then told them three prophecies. First, he told them that God would raise up those they saw as less than dirt to be children unto Abraham. Second, he told them one was coming after Him who would baptize in the Holy Ghost and fire. Thirdly, he told them there was coming a time when judgment would be poured out on the religious who did not produce fruit. These prophecies would be preaching the Full Gospel message of Salvation, Sanctification, Spirit Baptism, and the Second Coming. Before Jesus had even been properly introduced, John gave the mission, and in it, he included Spirit baptism and tied it with fire.

It should not have been a shock when the fire fell. They had been forewarned. But how do you prepare for something like that? We are in the Upper Room. We have been waiting at the place in which we have gotten used to waiting. All of a sudden, a sound that could have been almost deafening begins to erupt. The Bible talks about the sound without evidence of any actual wind. Just a sound from Heaven echoes through the room. While you are caught up in the sound, looking around at the ceiling, you see something you can only describe as flames falling on your neighbor. You look at them and they look at you. You see the same amazement on their face as you are experiencing in your spirit. This fire is sitting on you just like it is sitting on them. This was a sight, not a feeling. There was no proof there was any heat in this flame that could be felt with the skin, but it could be felt in the heart. There is no smoke or mirrors acquainted with this fire. This is the pure light of God shining forth for His children to see. The Holy Ghost baptism is a pure expression of love for His Church.

It was after the sight and sound of Pentecost that we were introduced to the sensation of Pentecost. This sensation is the only thing that will follow them out of the Upper Room. I am not saying it cannot happen, but we see no other Biblical passage of the sound or sight of Pentecost. The one thing they continued in was the sensation of speaking in tongues. God had been hinting at something they did not understand. Isaiah talked to them about stammering lips and another tongue, but they could not have understood what was happening from an Old Testament standpoint. They had heard about the wind and the fire, but this was a sensation they had no idea would happen. They had no idea when it was happening or the ramifications it would bring. Through this phenomenon, God would open them to a new way of praying and empowerment.

The New Testament walked out on the streets of Jerusalem an empowered Church. They would need this power to evangelize the world. They would also need this power to survive the persecution they would have to endure. This power is still needed for these two things. When appropriately used, the power of the Holy Ghost will reach the world with the Gospel of Jesus Christ. The power of God will also keep us amid intense persecution. When we hear about the power of the church of China and other places where Christianity is illegal, we also hear about persecution. God knows His Church will only survive persecution through His power. No one wants to be persecuted, but what an honor to be persecuted for our Lord and with our Lord. Just like the Hebrew boys were thrown into the fire, we are often thrown into situations of persecution. If you remember, the flames had no power over these boys to the point the smell of smoke had not even gotten in their clothes. When we go through the fire, we have the promise of Jesus that He fulfills by the Holy Ghost that He will be with us.

Psalm 91:1=4, "He that dwelleth in the secret place of the most High shall abide under the shadow of the Almighty. I will say of the LORD, He is my refuge and my fortress: my God; in Him will I trust. Surely He shall deliver thee from the snare of the fowler and from the noisome pestilence. He shall cover thee with His feathers, and under His wings shalt thou trust: His Truth shall be thy shield and buckler."

In the first four verses of Acts chapter 2, we are introduced to the power in its symbolism. I am not saying in any way that what happened in the Upper Room was not real. I believe everything that happened in the Upper Room was real. What I am saying is that God introduces us to the power in ways they can understand. Even today, these elements that represent the Holy Ghost are power producers. In John 11, Jesus shows us the Holy Ghost as water. In Acts 2, we are shown the Holy Ghost as wind and fire. These are elemental representatives of the Holy Ghost. What they have in common is they are all used to produce power. The water that runs over rocks produces hydrogen power. The wind powers the sails of a ship or even turn the mighty propellers wind farms producing power. Of course, the power produced by fire. Mix fire and water and you have steam - another form of power. Each of these elements is a power producer. God then, through tongues, gives us the sign of the Holy Spirit. In tongues, we are given another power producer.

Tongues do for our spirit man what lifting

weights does for our physical man. In 1 Corinthians 14, we are told that tongues were given to edify the spirit. I believe the more we pray in the Holy Ghost, the more God's power is produced in our lives. Read the life story of Smith Wigglesworth and you will see the importance he placed on speaking in tongues. Even the Apostle Paul testifies that he speaks in tongues more than anyone reading the Corinthian letter. If you look at all the great heroes of the Pentecostal faith and the great heroes of Acts, you will see the power produced in their lives by praying in the Spirit or speaking in tongues. We will move on in Acts 2, looking at the Empowered Church, but I want you to understand the turbine of power you have been given through praying in the Spirit/praying in tongues. Just as fire, water, and wind move the turbines naturally, tongues move the turbines in the spiritual.

Acts 2:5-8, "And there were dwelling at Jerusalem Jews, devout men, out of every nation under heaven. Now, when this was noised abroad, the multitude came together and were confounded because every man heard them speak in his language. And they were all amazed and marveled, saying one to another, Behold, are not all these which speak Galileans? And how to hear we every man in our own tongue, wherein we were born?"

In the early 1900s, shortly after the Azusa Street Revival began, people read this passage and thought speaking in tongues was primarily given to speak in other languages for missionary work. This has been one of those issues that has been misunderstood. Yes, on the Day of Pentecost, they indeed walked out of the Upper Room speaking in languages they had never learned. This phenomenon did gather the attention of all those who were there for the Feast of Pentecost. It is also true that, in this instance, speaking in tongues/languages got their attention because they could understand them in their own language. The Bible even gives a detailed list of those languages. What took place captured their attention, but Peter's message captured their hearts.

This is not saying that God cannot and has not used tongues to supernaturally speak to other people in a supernatural way. The best instance I know of that illustrates this was given by the great preacher and college president, Dr. Mark Rutland. Dr. Rutland tells the story of preaching in Japan to a large stadium full of Japanese people. He had been preaching with an interpreter who was conveying his message in the native tongue of that area. Some years earlier, God had supernaturally given Dr. Rutland the ability to speak Spanish. In this service, the Holy Spirit instructed Dr Rutland to give the altar call in Spanish. Here he was, preaching in English with the assistance of a Japanese interpreter, and God told him to give the altar call to a stadium full of Japanese people in Spanish. Dr. Rutland obeyed the Holy Ghost. I am sure it shocked him, shocked his interpreter, and confused the audience. All of a sudden, a beautiful dark-haired girl ran to the altar. She was the backslidden daughter of a Pentecostal preacher who had married a Japanese man and ran to Japan to get away from God. When she heard this altar call in her natural language, she knew the God she had run from had found her.

I am sure plenty of other random cases could be pointed out of something like this. My dad and mom had gone to pray for a dying lady. While Dad was praying for her, as he most often does, he started praying in tongues. While he was praying, a lady at the house who had studied languages recognized the language my dad was praying in. This was a witness to that lady. It bore witness to her concerning Christ, it bore witness concerning tongues, and it bore witness concerning my dad. God is big enough to do anything, anytime, for any reason He chooses to do so. We need to recognize when something is a supernatural act of God for a moment and an instance in time and when something has a pattern that can be seen as normal.

On the Day of Pentecost, the wind blew. We do not find another Biblical instance of wind blowing. I do know of testimonies of people hearing wind in a shut-up room while in a prayer meeting. It has happened, it can happen, and I believe it is happening. The sound of wind blowing is not normal. On the Day of Pentecost, forked flames were set upon each of them. There is no other Biblical sighting of this after the Day of Pentecost. Once again, there are testimonies of things like this happening. Floyd Lawhorn tells of being in Indonesia and what he could only describe as a ball of fire, yet it was not fire. It made its way all over the church and everyone it touched was filled with the Holy Ghost. It can happen, has happened, and is happening, but it is not normal. In the mouth of two or three witnesses, let it be established.

There is no other Biblical case for tongues to be used like this as a pattern or as normal. The other Acts passages of glossolalia do not include this. When Peter went to the house of Cornelius in Acts Chapter 10 and the Holy Ghost fell on the residents of Cornelius' house, they spoke in tongues, but there was no need for them to preach to Peter in tongues. There is also no indication that anyone in that house spoke a foreign language. They would have all spoken the same language. It is here that the idea that tongues were only given to preach in foreign languages falls apart. If we only had the Acts 2 account, we could conclude that tongues were a one-time thing and given to preach that one time to those people that day. Given the other Acts passages and the instruction of Paul in 1 Corinthians, tongues, as we know them and as the Bible supports them, are prayer languages to communicate with God and strengthen our spirit man. Tongues are powerful and God can use them in various ways, but the pattern set for tongues is more about prayer and less about preaching.

Acts 2:14-21, "But Peter, standing up with the eleven, lifted his voice, and said unto them, Ye men of Judaea, and all ye that dwell at Jerusalem, be this known unto you, and hearken to my words: For these are not drunken, as ye suppose, seeing it is but the third hour of the day. But this is that which was spoken by the prophet Joel; And it shall come to pass in the last days, saith God, I will pour out of My Spirit upon all flesh: and your sons and your daughters shall prophesy, and your young men shall see visions, and your old men shall dream dreams: And on My servants and on My handmaidens I will pour out in those days of My Spirit; and they shall prophesy: And I will shew wonders in heaven above, and signs in the earth beneath; blood, and fire, and vapor of smoke: The sun shall be turned into darkness, and the moon into blood, before the great and notable day of the Lord come: And it shall come to pass, that whosoever shall call on the name of the Lord shall be saved."

From the start of his mighty discourse that would be the first official message of the New Testament Church, Peter addresses the elephant on the street. He speaks to the supposed drunkenness of those leaving the Upper Room. I do not know what was happening, but whatever was happening made them appear to be drunk. In these few words in Acts 2:14, the groundwork for manifestations is laid. We know the Holy Ghost brings with Him gifts that He gives to His followers who have been empowered by His Spirit. These are the nine gifts that Paul deals with in 1 Corinthians. Before there were established gifts, there were manifestations. We can only guess what these might have been. Unlike the gifts of the Spirit, the manifestations of the Spirit are much more subjective. We do not have to have solid Scriptural evidence to make a case for them. They are also not to be used as a test of spirituality or have doctrine built around them as we do the gifts of the Spirit. (On a personal note, I have no issue with manifestations, but I have an issue with movements built around them.)

As far as I can tell, these manifestations are given because the physical body reacts to the God of Heaven touching it. I do not know of any other explanation. These manifestations, which the Pentecostal Movement has widely accepted for 120 years, seem to mimic intoxication to those outside the Pentecostal Movement. These manifestations can be traced through Pentecostal history and even hundreds of years before the Modern Day Pentecostal Movement. There are documented cases of manifestations in both the early Presbyterian and Methodist Movements. In the great campmeetings of the 1700s, it was recorded that people would fall out and that women's hair would pop like whips. Of course, we had an entire religious sect called the Quakers who would shake and quake when they were exposed to the presence of the Lord.

These are not drunk as you suppose. If a drunk man does it, we can assume this is what they saw on the streets that day that caused them to believe these people whom the Holy Ghost had touched were drunk. Drunk men cry. Possibly the most common manifestation is when the Spirit moves on people and they cry for seemingly no reason. It is simply the Spirit of God touching their emotions. Drunk men pass out. We have seen this happen thousands and thousands of times in the Pentecostal/Charismatic Church. Someone asked, "Why do they fall out?" The simple answer is they cannot stand up. I remember the first time I ever saw Dr. T. L. Lowery in person. I went to be prayed for and he barely touched me. When the tip of his finger hit my head, it was as if all the strength had been pulled from my body. I had no choice but to fall. Drunk men laugh. Drunk men dance. Drunk men do all sorts of things. Everything drunk men do, outside of cuss, I have seen manifested in the Church. I can't explain it. I can only say I love it!!! I love the manifestations of the Spirit and I desire to see and experience more of it.

As we take our last look at the Empowered Church, it is important to understand to whom this power is available. Remember that there was a definite hierarchy in the Jewish world of that day. This was one of the most discriminating times in human history and one of the discriminatory places during that time. When Peter stands and gives this message, it is more than beautiful poetry; it is actual prophecy. In these opening remarks of his message, he deals with every form of discrimination. This is something that would follow the move of the Holy Ghost throughout the centuries.

Peter begins this thought by quoting the Old Testament prophet, Joel. This would have been his text to his message. In the last days, God will pour out His Spirit upon all flesh. This does not mean every person walking, but every kind of flesh will be eligible for His Spirit. There is no color discrimination in the Holy Ghost. This was evident at Azusa Street when the Church became a melting pot. Peter gives a descriptive list of eligible people so there would be no doubt. Sadly, even with this list given by Peter, the Church was still discriminatory. Even Peter himself had to overcome this discrimination. There is no gender discrimination. He will pour His Spirit out on sons <u>and</u> daughters. There is no age discrimination. He will cause young <u>and</u> old to experience dreams and visions. There is no class discrimination. On servants and handmaidens, He will pour out His Spirit. The Holy Ghost is the Great Equalizer. Through the years, we have seen all these groups filled with the Holy Ghost and used mightily by the power of God.

    The first tone set for the New Testament Church is that it was then and should be now an Empowered Church. We could fill the rest of the pages of this book, along with volumes of books, examining all the known Biblical and historical cases of where the Church has experienced the supernatural power of God. The important thing to note is that the power is available to us. The expiration Peter placed on this dispensation of power is the great and notable day of the Lord's coming. This expiration date would match the date Paul set in 1 Corinthians 13 when he says these things will pass when that which is perfect has come. The "perfect" that is coming was not the canonization of the Bible. Though the Bible is perfect, our understanding of the Bible is not. The perfect thing Paul spoke about was not a thing, but a person. When Jesus returns in the clouds, Daniel's 70th week will begin and the Church age will end. The Holy Ghost will exit this earth, taking the true Church, the blood-bought redeemed, with Him.

1 Thessalonians 4:16-17, "For the Lord Himself shall descend from heaven with a shout, with the voice of the archangel, and with the trump of God: and the dead in Christ shall rise first: Then we which are alive and remain shall be caught up together with them in the clouds, to meet the Lord in the air: and so shall we ever be with the Lord."

Chapter 4:

"The Church Of Acts Was An Enthroned Church"

Acts 2:22-30, "Ye men of Israel, hear these words; Jesus of Nazareth, a man approved of God among you by miracles and wonders and signs, which God did by Him in the midst of you, as ye yourselves also know: Him, being delivered by the determinate counsel and foreknowledge of God, ye have taken, and by wicked hands have crucified and slain: Whom God hath raised up, having loosed the pains of death: because it was not possible that He should be holden of it. For David speaketh concerning Him, I foresaw the Lord always before my face, for He is on my right hand, that I should not be moved: Therefore did my heart rejoice, and my tongue was glad; moreover also my flesh shall rest in hope: Because Thou wilt not leave my soul in hell, neither wilt thou suffer Thine Holy One to see corruption. Thou hast made known to me the ways of life; thou shalt make me full of joy with thy countenance. Men and brethren, let me freely speak unto you of the patriarch David, that he is both dead and buried, and his sepulcher is with us unto this day. Therefore, being a prophet, and knowing that God had sworn with an oath to him, that of the fruit of his loins, according to the flesh, He would raise up Christ to sit on his throne.

As the Apostle Peter moves into his powerful message at Pentecost that will help bring order to the Church, he brings up King David. As already stated, this message connects the Savior to the Jewish people. Peter is laying out the groundwork for Jesus being the Messiah. If anyone is qualified for this task, it is Peter. Peter, by a sovereign act of the Father, is shown the greater identity of Jesus and, in this message, he is going to make that identity known to the thousands who will hear him preach that day. It is upon the rock of this revelation that God has established His Church. A revelation so powerful that the very gates of Hell could not prevail against this organism called the Church as long as it is built on this revelation. Keeping Matthew 16:18 in mind, it is only fitting that God would set the tone for the New Testament Church with this message.

Peter makes the case for Jesus being the King of Kings, but also for Jesus being the King of the Kingdom. The Church - which is the Body of Christ - is a part of the Kingdom. Think about it like this: the Kingdom of God is made up of the entire universe. Heaven, the celestial city, would be where the throne of God abides. Heaven is where The Father and the Son are currently seated in power. Note that in Acts 7:56, Stephen, at the time of his stoning, sees Jesus standing at the right hand of God. Peter has told us in Acts 2:33 that Jesus is seated at the right hand of God. In the third chapter, 22nd verse of his 1st book, Peter said, *"Who is gone into Heaven, and is on the right hand of God; angels and authorities and powers being made subject unto Him."* Heaven is the eternal city, the capitol of the Kingdom, and it is where the Father and Son rule and reign.

The Kingdom has a regional office made up of millions of branch offices on Earth. It is this earthly extension of the Kingdom that we call the Church. This earthly extension of the Kingdom has a Chief Executive

Officer who fully represents the royal family of Heaven. The CEO of the Earth extension of the Kingdom is the Holy Ghost. The Holy Ghost is the administrator of the Church and He represents the will of the Father and the Son in all matters concerning the Church. It is always the will of the Spirit to edify the Son and carry out the perfect will of Heaven. This is why praying in the Spirit is so important.

When we pray in the Spirit, we pray for the perfect will of God. When we pray in our understanding, we sometimes pray our will. The Spirit always, 100% of the time, is praying the will of the Father. The Holy Ghost has the final say on all decisions concerning The Church. This is why in Acts 15:28, the Church said, "It seemed good to the Holy Ghost and us..." If something does not seem good to the Holy Ghost, the true Church will have no part in it. The Holy Ghost has the only vote. He is not the chairman of the Church Board; He IS the Church Board. The Holy Ghost gets the only vote concerning matters of the Church. The spiritual elders always rubber-stamp the decision of the Holy Ghost, and the Spirit-controlled people in The Church never question it.

The carnal people in the Church are quick to question. Carnal people love to be heard. The great Pentecostal statesman and apostle of the last century, Rev. B. H. Clendennen, would say, "There is nothing in you that has a right. There is only something in you that wants a right." This is a struggle the Church has had from its inception. These carnal conflicts come about when the flesh of church people cry out to be heard. In Acts chapter 6, we see where flesh and carnal conflict is splitting the Church. Two different groups of widows are at odds. The conflict became so intense that the eternal spiritual work of the Church was being placed on hold. Finally, the Apostolic leadership of the Church rose to say, "Enough is enough! We were not called to referee fights among God's people. We cannot even study and pray because we have to deal so much with these conflicts." It is at this point they establish a new system of order. They decide to choose seven men full of wisdom and full of the Holy Ghost to carry out the day-by-day business of the Church. The fivefold ministry will be given over to prayer and study of the Word. This group will be in charge of carrying out the will of the Father concerning all things Spiritual and eternal. Then there will be a committee of deacons. This group will be responsible for carrying out the will of the Father concerning all this earthly and temporal. Note both groups are responsible for carrying out the will of the Father. This is why it is so important that our deacons, and even those making day-to-day decisions of the Church concerning its benevolence and physical ministry, should be filled with the Holy Ghost. If you are not filled with the Holy Ghost, how else will you know if it seems good to the Holy Ghost?

The Church is a theocracy, not a democracy. In a democracy, the majority rules. The decision getting the most votes has the final say. In a theocracy, only the King gets to vote. In the Church we have a King, and He has the only vote. The New Testament Church is an Enthroned Church where we have a King who makes His will known by His Spirit. His Spirit is subject to His

Word. His Spirit speaks His will through His prophets. His prophets are known by His call on their lives and the integrity of their walk with God. The Spirit of God has given us the Word of God and the Word of God is the plumbline. God will never violate His Word and His prophets will never violate His Word. His Spirit will agree with His will and those full of His Spirit will agree with His will. God is not the author of confusion and those who are full of the Holy Ghost with both the fruit of the Spirit and the gifts of the Spirit being present in their lives will not be confused by the Holy Ghost.

In his message, Peter establishes Jesus' right to be the King of this Kingdom. Jesus, being not only the Son of God but being of the same essence as God, thought it not robbery to be equal with God. Peter tells us that Jesus was chosen and appointed by God. God approved Jesus and God established who Jesus was among the people. Peter tells us that he and the other disciples are witnesses of these things and they are not simply cunning stories devised by clever men. All of salvation depends on the validity of Scripture. In order to come to God, you come by His Word and His Spirit. Both His Word and His Spirit point us to the divine nature of Christ. Peter is saying in the golden passage of this chapter that Jesus has full right to be the King of the Kingdom.

Rev 19:11-16, "And I saw heaven opened, and behold a white horse; and He that sat upon Him was called Faithful and True, and in righteousness, He doth judge and make war. His eyes were as a flame of fire, and on His head were many crowns, and He had a name written, that no man knew, but He Himself. And He was clothed with a vesture dipped in blood: and His name is called The Word of God. And the armies which were in heaven followed Him upon white horses, clothed in fine linen, white and clean. And out of His mouth goeth a sharp sword, that with it He should smite the nations: and He shall rule them with a rod of iron: and He treadeth the winepress of the fierceness and wrath of Almighty God. And He hath on His vesture and on His thigh a name written, KING OF KINGS, AND LORD OF LORDS."

Jesus Christ is the Eternal King of Kings and Lord of Lords. Jesus is the central figure of all of Christianity and He is the central figure of all of time and space. It is the honor and privilege of His Church to worship Him. There is not enough honor that can be bestowed on Him. Jesus cannot be over-emphasized, for it is not possible for Him to be emphasized enough. This is one reason why - though I disagree with the Oneness doctrine - I do not count them as a cult. If they did anything, they placed greater emphasis on Jesus and not less emphasis. The Mormons make Him one of many gods. They place Lucifer as His brothe, and He is simply a created being as you and I are. The Jehovah's Witnesses make Jesus simply Michael the Archangel. Once again, it is a cult that has lessened the place of Jesus. When we make Jesus less than eternal and less than deity and not the absolute, only means of salvation, we have abandoned Christianity. Christianity places Jesus at the center of it all. Jesus is not as the angels or as man; He was not a created being, but fully God. Jesus is the King of the Kingdom and one day, He will be recognized as the King of the World and the Universe!!!

A king is different from the president or the prime minister. These positions are elected positions. These positions are limited positions. These positions, for the most part, term out. A king is not elected by the people or by Parliament. If everyone in the kingdom decides they no longer want to serve the king, then they suffer the penalty of this. In this Kingdom, we suffer expulsion from the Kingdom. As long as you are in the Kingdom, you will serve and recognize the King. The King is not elected and cannot be voted out. The King has no limit to His power in a true Kingdom. In a true kingdom, the king has no term limit. He is king until he is no more. There are no three branches of government in a true kingdom. God's Kingdom is the true Kingdom. God answers to no one. God runs no decisions by anyone unless He so chooses. We cannot vote Jesus out and man cannot appeal or amend His decrees.

We live in a time where a rewriting of history is being attempted. This is just a step to rewrite and change the Bible. The Bible is not like the IPHC Manual or COG Minutes. The Bible is not even like the United

States Constitution. It cannot be changed, it cannot be amended, it cannot be dissolved, and it cannot be canceled. Heaven and Earth will pass away, but His Word shall never pass away. If the entire Church decided today that the Bible was no longer true and what it says is outdated, it would still be just as accurate. The Bible is absolute. The Bible holds all spiritual and moral authority. The Bible is headed where it is headed, and there are no course adjustments to the Bible. The Bible can no more change that the location of Israel could change. When the Children of Israel were following the cloud, the cloud, which was the presence of God, was going to the Promised Land. If all of Israel had decided to change course and the entire camp, including Moses, decided the Promised Land was in another direction, the Promised Land would still be where it was and the cloud would still be going there. If God had said to all His people to turn around and walk away, He would not have chased them down and started following them. God will not change course today - no matter how they try to rewrite or reinterpret the Bible.

The question comes, "How does one become King?" The way I see it, there are three ways one can become King. Number one, you are king by lineage. You were born into royalty and when the time comes, if you are in line for the throne, you are made king. Jesus was King by lineage. Peter traces the lineage of Jesus back to that of David. In Peter's message at Pentecost, Peter establishes Jesus as the rightful heir to this throne. We can see through the genealogies that Jesus stands in line to take the throne of David. The way this type of king works is that they must prove they are in line to be king. If one can come forward who can prove they have a better claim to the throne, then they can overtake the Kingdom.

Jesus has a solid claim to the throne of David. Jesus has the lineage to prove it. Keeping this in mind, others, after this many years, could challenge Jesus for the throne. They would be wrong, but the challenge could be made. Jesus has no rival of lineage when it comes to the throne of David. Before David was King and before Saul was King, Israel had another King. God told Samuel that He was content to be their King, but they rejected God as their King in rejecting God's judge and prophetic voice, Samuel. Jesus was not only King by the lineage of David, but more importantly, Jesus was King by the lineage of God. Jesus, being both the son of David and the Eternal Son of God, has the right to the throne by lineage.

*Luke 1:31-33, "And, behold, thou shalt conceive in thy womb, and bring forth a son, **<u>and shalt call His name JESUS</u>**. **<u>He shall be great</u>**, **<u>and shall be called the Son of the Highest</u>**: **<u>and the Lord God shall give unto Him the throne of His father David</u>**: And He shall reign over the house of Jacob forever, and of His Kingdom,<u> there shall be no end</u>."*

John 1:1-3, "In the beginning was the Word, and the Word was with God, and the Word was God. The same was in the beginning with God. He made all things, and without Him was not anything made that was made."

Gen 1:26, "And God said, <u>Let Us make man in Our image, after Our likeness</u>: ..."

John 8:58, "Jesus said unto them, Verily, verily, I say unto you, Before Abraham was, I am."

The second way a king is chosen is he becomes king by virtue. When kings were being set forth in the formation of kingdoms, they were chosen by acts of virtue. Remember the story of King Arthur when he pulled the sword out of the stone and this act made him the King of Camelot? Though this is a fictitious story, it illustrates how a king becomes a king by virtue. Jesus had the right to be King not only by lineage, but also by virtue. What more virtuous act could one do than to pay a price they do not owe for someone they do not know? That is exactly what Jesus did for you and me. *"He paid a debt He did not owe, I owed a debt I could not pay, I needed someone to wash my sins away, and now I sing a brand new song, Amazing Grace, Christ Jesus paid the debt that I could never pay."* ("He Paid A Debt"; Ellis J. Crum; 1977) His death on the cross of Calvary was the greatest act of virtue ever done by anyone. I cannot praise Him enough, honor Him enough, or obey Him enough for what He did for me. I gladly say He is my King.

*Rev 5:2-5, "And I saw a strong angel proclaiming with a loud voice, **Who is worthy to open the book, and to loose the seals thereof**? **And no man in Heaven, nor in earth, neither under the earth, was able to open the book, neither to look thereon**. **And I wept much because no man was found worthy to open and to read the book, neither to look thereon**. And one of the elders saith unto me, **Weep not**: **behold, the Lion of the tribe of Juda, the Root of David, hath prevailed to open the book, and to loose the seven seals thereof**."*

*Rev 4:10-11, "The four and twenty elders fall down before Him that sat on the throne, and worship Him that liveth forever and ever, and cast their crowns before the throne, saying, Thou **art worthy, O Lord**, to **receive glory and honor and power**: **for Thou hast created all things**, and for Thy pleasure they are and* *were created."*

The final way we will deal with how one becomes king is by conquest. Kings are often made when an army dethrones another king or simply conquers a people. This may be by a great general who conquers a land and is elevated to king. It may be by the king of another nation who conquers a new nation. Jesus has the right to be King by lineage. Jesus has the right to be King by virtue. Jesus also has the right to be King by being a conqueror, for Jesus has conquered things no other can conquer. It is one thing to conquer a land or a people, but it is a whole other thing to conquer Death and Hell. Yet Jesus, the King of Kings, has done just that.

Jesus conquered death when a frantic father came to Him and asked Him to come to heal his sick daughter. This little girl had just passed when they arrived at the man's house. Jesus commands all doubters to leave. He pulls out the same power He used to create the worlds and, by His voice, commands her to arise.

Jesus, finding a funeral procession with a young man on his way to be buried, lays His hand on the casket and conquers death. Then we see that Jesus' best friend has been dead for four days and is already in the grave, body stinking, and Jesus once again utilizes the weapon of His voice and says, "Lazarus, *come forth.*" Jesus conquered death in all its stages: Before the body is even cold or the funeral director has been called; On the way to the graveyard in the middle of the funeral (I am unsure if the funeral director gave a refund or a discount!); After the funeral director has been paid and gone home. Even with all these victories, none of them will compare to when He is going to conquer death for all the sainted dead. With this, He is going to conquer sin and Satan. He will be *"the all-time undisputed, undefeated Champion of Love."* ("Champion of Love"; Carolyn Cross, Phil Cross; 1987) There will be no question. He is King - and He is King by conquest.

The New Testament Church does not need Jesus' birth certificate to call Him King. This Church does not need to see any greater act of virtue to call Him King.

There is coming a day that every knee will bow and tongue confess that He is King. For the New Testament Church, He is King now. We do not need anyone to bow our knees. Our knees freely and happily bow to Him at the mention of His name. The New Testament Church is an Enthroned Church.

Rev 20:1-2, "And I saw an angel come down from heaven, having the key of the bottomless pit and a great chain in his hand. <u>*And he laid hold on the dragon*</u>*, that old serpent,* <u>*which is the Devil, and Satan, and bound him a thousand years*</u>*,"*

Chapter 5:

"The Church Of Acts Was An Evangelistic Church"

Acts 2:37-41, *"Now when they heard this, they were pricked in their heart, and said unto Peter and to the rest of the apostles, Men, and brethren, what shall we do? Then Peter said unto them, Repent, and be baptized every one of you in the name of Jesus Christ for the remission of sins, and ye shall receive the gift of the Holy Ghost. For the promise is unto you, and to your children, and to all that are afar off, even as many as the LORD our God shall call. And with many other words did he testify and exhort, saying, Save yourselves from this untoward generation. Then they that gladly received his word were baptized: and the same day there were added unto them about three thousand souls."*

The New Testament Church was infused with power for one primary purpose. It was the will of Christ for His Church to carry out the Great Commission.

Looking back at all the passages in the Gospels and Acts chapter 1, you will see Jesus' charge to carry out this commission. You will also see His promise of power. When we see these two things together so profoundly, we must note that they are connected. The obvious conclusion we will arrive at is the outpouring of the Holy Spirit is given to carry out the Great Commission. The Great Commission is twofold: make converts and make disciples. Get people saved and then get people serving. These are not two separate commands, but rather two sides of the same coin.

The reason I say something that should be so obvious is modern evangelism has lost this understanding. So many feel their only responsibility is to get people to say the prayer. These people are often zealous and the first to share their faith, but they can also be very destructive to the true advancement of the Kingdom. In addition, it can be very deceptive to the one who has prayed the prayer. This deception is dangerous for it leaves people with a skewed understanding of salvation. It is also dangerous because it can deliver false security. The Great Commission is in no way charging people to talk others into praying a prayer and then deeming them saved. The Great Commission calls people to repentance. This is a call to leave your old way of doing and thinking and walk in a Biblical worldview/Holiness. This is a call to death and it is a call to the newness of life in Christ led by the Holy Spirit. In the waters of baptism, we play out in plain sight what has already happened in the heart. We go under the water full of self and flesh. The water symbolizes the ground just as a body dies and is laid under the dirt. We come out of the water a new creation in Christ just as we will one day arise from the grave with a glorified body.

Once this act of baptism has played out, we rise from our watery grave. Our new life in Christ has begun when we leave the waters of baptism. Old things have passed away, and all things have become new. We are truly new creations in Christ Jesus. It is here that the "observe all things whatsoever I have commanded you" part kicks in. Once one is resurrected through faith in

Christ and converted by the power of the Holy Spirit, they are redeemed. The sign of resurrection is not the water dripping from their clothes, but rather the hunger that comes with true resurrection. When Jesus raised Jairus' daughter from the dead, He immediately commanded that she should be fed. When one has transformed from spiritual death to spiritual life, we – the Church – must feed them. Furthermore, they will be hungry. Real conversion brings real hunger. The newly converted will not be perfect, but they will be hungry. If you ever find yourself lacking in hunger, take a trip to the altar. Stay and pray until you get hungry again for the presence of God in your life.

The way we have done evangelism in the last decades is the equivalent of a lady having a baby and throwing it in a ditch. The lady then leaves the place where she gave birth and brags about how she just gave birth. The first question should be, "Where is the baby?" She should be arrested if she cannot tell you where that baby is. When people make wild claims of all the souls they have won to the Kingdom, the statement that should follow is, "I want to see the baby." If they cannot show you the baby/newly converted, they should be arrested for child neglect. Evangelism is hard work when it is coupled with discipleship, and it is a fraud when it is not. When the Holy Spirit has uses me to bring the message of Christ into another life, I must then either take responsibility for that life or hand them off to one who can. I am not saying to not share your faith. I am not saying to not pray with people. We need to do all those things and project the seed of God's Word everywhere we go. Most churches have lost true evangelism. Often, it has been lost by the most zealous among us.

The altar calls of the last century have added to this confusion about evangelism. I have often said the "Sinner's Prayer" is one of the worst things to happen to the Church. I am sure when this was first proposed, it was to be a tool to help streamline Scripture concerning salvation. What it became was a lazy way to get people "saved." Then, when the full brunt of the "Once Saved, Always Saved" doctrine kicked in, it produced generations of so-called Christians who do not know God. My great problem with this "prayer" is that it is not how Jesus gave altar calls or how the New Testament Church applied salvation. Neither Jesus nor His New Testament ministers took the lazy way out. Their instruction concerning salvation did not mirror our instruction of today. There was no bowing your head, no one looking around, every eye closed, and we would slip you into the Kingdom. They were out and they were loud. When someone got saved, everyone knew they had been radically transformed. Does the Gospel we preach to the people we reach bring about conversion?

2 Corinthians 5:17-20, "Therefore if any man be in Christ, he is a new creature: old things are passed away; behold, all things are become new. And all things are of God, who hath reconciled us to Himself by Jesus Christ, and hath given to us **the ministry of reconciliation***; To wit, that God was in Christ, reconciling the world unto Himself, not imputing their trespasses unto them; and hath committed unto us* **the**

Word of reconciliation. *Now then we are ambassadors for Christ, as though God did beseech you by us: we pray you in Christ's stead,* ***be ye reconciled to God.***"

When one is born again, they are reborn into someone and something they previously were not. The Apostle Paul tells us we have been given the task of reconciliation. He then tells us the standard of reconciliation. He follows this by making it crystal clear that we are being reconciled to God and not God being reconciled to us. There is a major difference. The modern evangelist is often working to reconcile God to man. We do this when we do not present the whole story. When we preach a God who makes allowances for sin and does not care how you live as long as you believe, we produce what we have today. I call it "Southern Christianity". It is a fraudulent adaptation of Biblical Christianity. It is what the early Catholic leaders did when they took the gods of the pagans and gave them the names of the saints. They mixed the Bible with idolatry and produced a God reconciled to them. When the modern church preaches a sinning religion that makes no demands of conforming to the Word of God, we have reconciled God to man rather than reconciling man to God.

When Jesus gave an altar call, His altar call was much different. He did not say, "Come unto Me and I will pay your bills." He did not say, "Come unto Me and life will be easier for you." He did not say, "Repeat after Me and you will be as saved as if you were already in Heaven." No, that is not what Jesus said. Those are some things we say. We stand before people and, like a car salesman, we try to sell people our product. I have heard it said and have probably said myself, "Just try Jesus. If you do not like Him, the Devil will always take you back." Though I know that is a little funny, it does embrace our thinking. "You have tried everything else. Give Jesus a try." Jesus is not an ice cream flavor to be tried. Jesus is the total ratification of one's life. When you come to Jesus, you are not giving Him a try to see if you like Him. Right up front, He tells you what He has to offer and then, with all that, you decide to die to the flesh and be born to the Spirit.

This was how Jesus gave His altar call or His appeal to the lost. He tells a man who is very rich that if he wants to be His, he needs to sell all he has, give it to the poor, and follow Him. He tells a woman caught in the act of adultery that He does not condemn her, but then He gives the instructions to go and sin no more. When giving out His mass altar call, He tells them that if they are not willing to give up their mother, father, sister, brother, and their own lives, they are not worthy to follow Him. Jesus appeals to them to take up their cross and follow Him. Jesus says to those looking for salvation that those who endure to the end shall be saved. Jesus never once sugar-coated His call to those desiring to be His followers. I am not saying to do your best to discourage people from following Christ. I am saying to be honest and preach what the Bible says.

The New Testament Church was an Evangelistic Church, and they turned the world upside down. They did not use games and gimmicks to do it. They did not make empty promises. They preached the message Jesus preached and taught the lessons Jesus taught. The altar call of the New Testament did not look like the ones of the modern Church, nor did Jesus' appeal. The way the New Testament Church saved someone was a total life transformation. There is no use of the "sinner's prayer" or the lifting of a hand while all eyes are closed. The Bible says that they received the Word. The Word they received was the Word that Peter preached at Pentecost. They received the revelation that Jesus is God and all the Apostles preached about Jesus. Once they received the Word, they were then baptized. They followed Christ in death and resurrection. Then the Bible says they joined themselves to the Church. The Church and following Christ became their life. I tell you now that this is what salvation still looks like. It is when one accepts all the Bible teaches about Jesus and then gives their entire life to learning of Him and following Him in obedience to His Word.

We have been called to be reconciled to God. We need to know what reconciliation is. If I have a clock on my oven that says the time is 9:09, but I know my oven clock is off, I can check with the satellite connected to my phone. This time is accurate and is always reconciled to the satellite it is connected to. The phone will even reconcile to the correct time if I change time zones. Now, if I want my oven time reconciled to the right time, I check what the phone says and adjust the time on the oven clock. I cannot reconcile my phone to the wrong time, for it is built into the phone to always reconcile to the satellite.

The Bible is the Word of Reconciliation. The Bible is reconciled to the will of God in Heaven. If I want my life and the lives of those to whom I minister to be reconciled with God, I must present to them the Word of Reconciliation. The greatest ministry of the New Testament Church is bringing lives into reconciliation with God. This is what true Evangelism is. It is not a one-time event. It is a lifetime work. After being both a pastor and evangelist for over 30 years, I can tell you it is hard work. It is often thankless work and, even more sad, it can seem fruitless.

One morning, my secretary came to me and said,

"There is a lady who has reached out to the church and I feel you should go see her." She went on to say, "She feels her brother is tormented with demons and she needs a preacher who can pray." I arrived at the home of these people. I had never seen them or spoken to them in my life. They had moved to South Carolina from the mountains of Virginia. The young lady and her brother had attended a Pentecostal church with their great-grandparents. They knew the only hope they had was someone who could touch Heaven. They had several little dogs in the house they had put in a back room. The entire time I worked to minister to this family, these little dogs barked and barked. The Spirit of God shone through in the middle of the darkness over that home. The presence of the Lord filled that room, and those little dogs calmed down. God had met with us and we prayed prayers of deliverance and surrender.

You would have thought that after the move of God that took place in that room, these folks would have been in church the next day. You would have thought wrong. It took me two years of visiting that family, praying for them, and going to the hospital with them before they ever showed up at my church. It was after they came that the real work began. This is the long, hard work of evangelism. It is so much more than saying a prayer and walking away.

New Testament evangelism is day by day, house by house. The fun part of being a pastor is preaching. I love to preach. I love to have good church services. The hard part of being a pastor is the pastor part. It is being there on the bad days and being that shoulder to cry on. It is playing ref to carnal church members who should be long past spiritual infancy. If you are not willing to stay up all night with a sick child, then do not become a parent. If you are not willing to walk someone through the trials of life and, at the very least, hand them off to a church family who will love them and will raise them, do not birth spiritual children. Far too many modern evangelists are birthing babies for abortion. The wolves of this world are devouring them because we love the preaching side of ministry and have forsaken the pastoral side of ministry. The fun part of seeing a new baby born must be saddled with the work part of making bottles and changing diapers. There are just as many midnight feedings with new converts as there are with newborn babies.

Acts 2 sets the tone for the New Testament Church regarding evangelism. We see one of the largest harvests ever gathered at a single setting in holy writ. It was a successful day, it was a joyous day, and it was a day that was to be duplicated throughout the Church Age. One of the reasons this point was so vital on this day was because of the Jews. Jews did not evangelize. They grew through generational growth. They grew by having children. They were both a people and a religion. For Peter to come with a message of conversion reflecting Jesus' message of conversion was something new to the Jews. They would have to reroute their thinking and start seeing every lost person as a potential person for salvation. This understanding would expand as the years passed and the pages of Acts would bring us this record. They would go from only reaching unsaved Jews to reaching the entire world. It did not happen on this day, but it set the tone for the days, weeks, months, and years to come.

This Church of today needs to revisit this tone set by Acts chapter 2. We, like the Jews of that day, do not evangelize. We often try to grow our churches through generational growth. We grow by having babies. If we can just get enough people in our church to have babies, we will grow the church. I have a dear friend who had 13 children and six grandchildren. Some of his grandchildren are older than his children. They are often teased that they bring church growth everywhere they go. I have heard it said that if we just held onto our children, we would double every ten years. Sadly, there are a lot of churches that this is their growth strategy. The truth is we do need to evangelize our homes. We do need to reach and disciple our children. As important as that is, we need to be a reaching church. Our method of church growth must be more than having babies. There is a lost world and we have been called to go into it and reach it. Not at the expense of abandoning our children, but bringing our children with us to reach the lost.

We recently did a three-day outdoor crusade in our town. Before the crusade, thousands of fliers were printed and distributed throughout our area. One day before the crusade began, around 40 of us hit the streets preaching the Gospel and passing out fliers. Part of that 40 were 16 children ages 4 to 19. These young men and women ran from person to person, passing out fliers and asking them to come to the revival. My youngest daughter, Emmelyn Grace Nail, who is nine years old at the time of this writing, was part of that group. I will never forget the expression on her face when she ran to me to tell me someone had taken that flier out of her hand. You would have thought she had personally snatched a soul from Hell! You do not have to go to a foreign nation to be a missionary or to take your youth on a mission trip. Right where you are, there is a mission field, and you are already armed with an army of your children and young people. As wonderful as the crusade in the park was, the greatest thing that happened that week was to see our children engage in the harvest.

The New Testament Church was multigenerational. Peter had already set the tone when he quoted from the prophet Joel concerning who was eligible to be used by God. Our children are the standard of what we should be doing. This is why Jesus says we must become little children to enter the Kingdom. Small children will teach you how to be a Christian if you allow them to.

When my son, Collin, was about 5 or 6 years old, he was taking his bath. I went in where he was in his mother's large bathtub, covered in bubbles. I started helping him get the suds out of his hair, and he started talking to me about our neighbors who had just moved in behind us. He said, "Daddy, our new neighbors are really nice, but they do something I do not like." I asked him, "What is that?" Collin said, "They smoke." I asked, "Did you give them an invite card and ask them to attend church?" Collin said, "No, I did not." He then jumped up out of the bath and hurried off. A few minutes later, he comes from the back in a pair of orange shorts and a Clemson Tigers shirt. He had tucked that shirttail into those shorts and combed his hair straight back. He looked like an old-time Church of God evangelist from his neck up. Like little David armed with a sling, he took his armor with him. He had his Bible under one arm and an invite card in the other hand. By his side was his 4-year-old sister. I said, "Collin, it is dark outside; those people will not want you showing up at their door." Then he said something that will always stick in my mind, "Daddy, I need to go, I must go." They went and came back with big smiles on their little faces. I asked, "What did they say?" Collin said, "They told us to go home." That response did not discourage him. Collin had done what he must do. May this be the attitude of the New Testament Christian, "I MUST GO!!!"

Luke 14:23, "And the lord said unto the servant, Go out into the highways and hedges, and compel them to come in, that my house may be filled."

Chapter 6:

"The Church Of Acts Was An Engaged Church"

Acts 2:42-43, *"And they continued steadfastly in the apostles' doctrine and fellowship, and in breaking of bread, and in prayers. And fear came upon every soul: and many wonders and signs were done by the apostles."*

Jesus commanded His Church to be two things. Jesus told His Church to be salt and to be light. He also told them that they were in this world, but not of this world. As we start this chapter, I want to make clear what I am **not** saying. I am not saying the Church was called to be engaged in this world's financial and political system. As Pastor Loran Livingston – pastor of the 10,000 member Central Church of God in Charlotte, North Carolina – would say, "This is not our world." We have not been called to rehabilitate this world. Our calling is not to engage the systems of a fallen world. Our calling is to engage the society of that world. We engage this society with two things: the Word of God and the power of God. This is done in three ways according to the foundational text of this chapter.

We engage society through doctrine. Doctrine is preaching and teaching. The tone is being set as to how the Church is engaged. When we think about something being engaged, I think about engaging an engine. The tiny spark produced by the spark plug engages that engine and brings it to life. Through the power of teaching and preaching, the world we live in is engaged in the power of God. Derek Prince, possibly the greatest Bible teacher of the last 100 years, says Jesus gave His Church the mode or the method in which it is to engage the world, "Preach the Gospel, heal the sick, and cast out devils." He goes on to say that when we think there is another way, we are trying to improve on Christ's way. We see from the start this is the tone set for the New Testament Church. There is still nothing more effective to engage the world than preaching the Gospel.

They would go daily into the temple and preach the Gospel. Though I think it is wonderful to preach everywhere, the most effective place to preach the

Gospel is in the church house for regular church services. The church is where people come to hear the Word. It is where they know they are going to hear the Word. Even the sinner knows when they go to church that the Gospel is going to be preached. With this understanding, their hearts will be most open to hearing the Gospel in a revival or regular scheduled religious service. This is why I think you will often find Jesus and the disciples preaching in the Temple and synagogues. They knew people were there to be engaged by the Scriptures. We waste time in our church services when we do not use that precious time to preach the doctrine of Christ. We are called to engage our audience with the Gospel of Jesus Christ and the Word of God – not some 12-step psychology lesson. It is almost as if the Church has become bored of Jesus and is looking for something else to engage people with. Take advantage of that most precious hour of the week that you have been given to tell the grand story and infuse lives with the Gospel of Christ.

Believe it or not, there are also times when we

need to be stealthy with our engagement of the human heart. Funerals are a wonderful place to engage the heart, but also a place where we can take advantage of the situation. I have seen preachers abuse the situation. When we preach at a funeral, we are called to comfort a family and try to say nice things about the person lying in the casket. If we take this opportunity to simply preach a Gospel message, we have done a disservice to that family and really to our Lord. As preachers, we need to read the room.

I have preached more funerals than I can count. Most of those funerals were for people I did not know. My church was across the street from a funeral home when I lived in Pensacola. They called on me to do all the funerals of people who had no preacher. For them to call me meant they did not know a preacher and no one in their immediate family knew a preacher. Those families were at least two generations removed from Biblical Christianity. Yet they were still Christian enough that they wanted a preacher to do their loved one's service. I could have gone in with Gospel guns blazing. I could have preached and held that family for 30 minutes, quoting Bible verses. That is not why they were there. When we take advantage of people's hearts and time, a service can quickly become a hostage situation. Many preachers have held their audience hostage and accomplished nothing but to make them mad.

I once was called to preach a funeral for a man I had never met. I called the family and collected as much information about the man as possible. There was not much to say about his goodness or accomplishments. The only thing that stood out was his heart for cats. He took in lost and abandoned cats. I preached a message I called "God Collects Strays". In a 10 to 15-minute space of time, I did everything I could to honor that man and then took a few minutes to talk about how God also collects strays. I was not there to explain all the fine points of redemption or preach holiness. I have Sunday mornings to do that to those who know what they are walking into. On this day, I was there to honor a life and point people to Jesus.

As we engage society, let us learn how to engage people. The call is to be salt and light. This means we are called to make people thirsty and to flavor the Gospel. Not water it down, but flavor it. We need to live and speak in such a way that people become thirsty just by being around us.

Sometimes I go off to Walmart or the local grocery store in my small town on a mission. My mission for that day is to be salt and light. I am not there passing out Gospel tracks or with a megaphone preaching in the parking lot. I am there armed with a smile and a nod. I simply walked through that store, being nice. Being nice goes a long way. While in these places, opportunities will open for you to engage those who need the Lord. I was in the self-checkout at Walmart last week when I heard a lady say, "That is the pastor right there." A couple was standing there with a Walmart employee and she was talking to them about the Lord. They said to her, "Did you have this planned?" No, she did not have it planned, but the Lord did. Right in the middle of Walmart, I took that couple by the hands, prayed for them, and invited them to our church. This is a simple example of being salt and light.

The Gospel flows out of actions of kindness. I learned this as a teenager before I ever started preaching. I was in the hospital with my parents where we had been visiting the sick. This was something we often did when I was a child growing up. Just being salt and light to those in need. On our way out of the hospital, there was a man in a wheelchair who was about to go through a heavy door. It was a large door, and he was in a wheelchair. I ran up in front of him and pulled the door open for him. I simply smiled and nodded at him when he was out the door. This man looked up at me and said, "You must be a Christian." To this day, it was the greatest compliment I have ever received. This man looked at a teenage boy and saw Christ. The Apostle Paul said, "And they glorified God in me." This should be the goal of every Christian every day: that those with whom we come in contact would glorify God in us. As B. H. Clendennen said, "We are just containers that carry the life of Christ.

Jesus also called us to be light in this dark world. Just as we have been called to make people thirsty to know the Lord, we have been called to shine the way for people to know Him. Our lives should be illuminated to all who see us. The light of God's Word should live in us and constantly shine in us. One of my favorite songs from my days in children's church was "This Little Light of Mine". My favorite part of that song was "Hide it under a bushel? No! I'm gonna let it shine." We are a city set on a hill and if Christ is in us, it should not be hidden. The real question concerning engagement is not how many Bible verses you can quote or how many rules you keep, but does your life point people to Christ? Are you a beacon shining in the dark? You don't need to run for public office, march on the streets, or start a Facebook campaign to be a light. Just try smiling and allowing the fruit of the Spirit to be so heavy on you that someone can smell the aroma of that fruit when you walk into a room.

When the children of Israel were taken captive into Babylon, none of them were happy about the situation. Many rose up as if they were speaking for God and told them that God would take them back home immediately. As a result of these false prophecies, the children of Israel decided to sit down and not be compliant. They decided they would be disruptive by doing nothing until they were delivered from that place. God, through the prophet Jeremiah, rose up and rebuked them. He tells them not to listen to their prophets and diviners, for God has not spoken to or sent them. The next thing God says to the exiled captives of Israel applies to us and teaches the Church how to be salt and light.

Jeremiah 29:4-7, "Thus saith the L<small>ORD</small> *of hosts, the God of Israel, unto all that are carried away captives, whom I have caused to be carried away from Jerusalem unto Babylon; Build ye houses, and dwell in them; and plant gardens, and eat the fruit of them; Take ye wives, and beget sons and daughters; and take wives for your sons, and give your daughters to husbands, that they may bear sons and daughters; that ye may be increased there, and not diminished. And seek the peace of the city whither I have caused you to be carried away captives, and pray unto the LORD for it: for in the peace thereof shall ye have peace."*

God first says to them, "I am the reason you are here." We will sometimes rebuke the devil when God places us in the middle of where we are. God put us in the World for a reason. God put you where you are for a reason. If we are not careful, we can curse our harvest by resenting where God placed us. God has you in your community to engage that community with the life of Christ. I have friends who pastor much, much larger churches than I pastor. They also pastor much, much wealthier people than I pastor. Part of this is because they live in much larger cities with much wealthier people. If I am not careful, I can get my eyes on their situation and forget that God put me where I am and put them where they are. Never be resentful of your mission field. To resent where God placed you is to be resentful of God.

Once you get to the point of accepting where you

are by the plan of God, you are then ready to move on in God's plan. One of my early mentors use to say, "You cannot build a church with leaving on your mind." You cannot properly engage a community with leaving on your mind. Establishing proper ministry and the people's confidence to engage a community takes time. This comes from spending time in that community. Marrying their children, burying their dead, praying over their businesses - this is the engagement they need to see out of us. If you can take the heat and do the time, there will come a time when they will see you as the town's pastor.

Just today, on the morning of this writing, my wife's best friend was taking our children to school. She is a lawyer and an officer of the court. She got pulled over on her way to the school. She said the officer was not happy with her because she drove a half mile after he turned his blue lights on. She said she thought he could have taken her to jail for failure to comply. He looked at her driver's license and said, "That address looks familiar." He then asked her if that was "the preacher's house?" She replied, "No, but that is the preacher's daughter in the back seat. I was running late taking them to school." The officer came back with a warning and a kind and sweet demeanor. I do not even know who this officer was, but somewhere in the past 16 years, I had positively engaged him.

The Church can be anarchists or we can do what God told the children of Israel to do and engage our society in a way that represents Him. What God was saying to Israel was to be a blessing wherever you go. Leave peace and not war. The Spirit of the Lord is in you to do more than speak in tongues and perform miracles. The Spirit of the Lord is for you to make bitter water sweet. There is nothing more sweet than the presence of the Lord at work in His children. The atmosphere should change as we walk into a room. The Spirit of the Lord in us should subdue the spirit of the world at work in that room. This is not a religious spirit, but a righteous spirit. As Paul put it in 2 Corinthians chapter 5, verse 20: *"Now then we are ambassadors for Christ, as though God did beseech you by us..."* Is God engaging people through you for them to come to Him?

Many years ago, my brother-in-law died very unexpectedly. I was in revival in Dayton, Tennessee, when I got the call. I had not been close to him for many years, but he was my nephew's father, and I loved my nephew like he was my own child. I flew to Norfolk, Virginia, thinking I was going there to be with my sister and 8-year-old nephew. After I arrived there, I realized I was there for my brother-in-law's family. Every night, the living room would fill with family members as I would expound the Word of God. My sister told me, "Tim, I did not know you knew all that." I told her I didn't know all that. The Holy Ghost was working through me. My brother-in-law attended and was a member of First Baptist Church in Norfolk. The pastor of that massive church did the funeral. On the way back to the family's house, I rode with my brother-in-law's sister and her family. His sister asked me, "Tim, I am not saying you are God, but why is it when you are around, it feels as if God is around? When you walk into a room, it is as if God walked into the room? When you get in the car, it is like God just got in the car. Why do I not feel that coming out of Thomas' pastor?" I told her, "That is the Holy Spirit you are feeling." The Holy Spirit engaged that family. I was simply the container He worked in.

Everywhere the child of God goes, the Spirit of God goes. When Jacob went to live with his Uncle Laban, God blessed Laban's house. God blessed Laban because of Jacob. God blessed Laban so much that he was willing to use his own daughters as pawns to keep Jacob as his employee. When Joseph was sold into slavery, he rose to the head of Potiphar's house and God blessed the house just because Joseph was in it. When Joseph went to prison, he rose to the head of the prison. He eventually became the administrative head of Egypt and, due to his presence and position, the entire nation and region was spared from death. This is how we engage a society. We are productive, and we pray for the peace of that society. America is blessed because of the Christians. The world is blessed because of the blood-bought, Holy Ghost baptized Church. The day is soon coming when we will be called away and the restrainer of sin and judgment will be removed.

"Until then, my heart will go on singing. Until then, with joy, I'll carry on. Until the day my eyes behold that city, until the day God calls me home." (Stuart Hamblen; Hamblen Music Company, 1958)

This is what the Engaging Church should be doing. We should be productive. We should be planting fields and eating what they produce. We should be building houses and living in them. We should be getting married and having children. I know we live in a fallen world. I know this world is getting so bad, it would be tempting to head to the hills and hide out. God called us to engage this world. We cannot win the world by being like the world. We cannot win the world by hiding from the world. We must be engaged in everyday society. Walking in doctrine, walking in fellowship, and walking in power. Three things have been given to us to engage the world. We have been given the knowledge to engage the world with the Word of God. We have been given the personality to engage with the world with the fruit of the Spirit. We have been given the power to engage this world with gifts of the Spirit. Not only do we need to evangelize, but we also need to engage. The tone set for the New Testament Church was for it to be an Engaging Church.

Acts 17:22-23, "Then Paul stood in the midst of Mars hill and said, Ye men of Athens, I perceive that in all things ye are too superstitious. For as I passed by, and beheld your devotions, I found an altar with this inscription, TO THE UNKNOWN GOD. Whom therefore ye ignorantly worship, **Him declare I unto you.***"*

Chapter 7:

"The Church Of Acts Was An Embracing Church"

Acts 2:44-46, "And all that believed were together, and had all things common; And sold their possessions and goods, and parted them to all men, as every man had need. And they, continuing daily with one accord in the temple, and breaking bread from house to house, did eat their meat with gladness and singleness of heart,"

The tone of the New Testament was one of family and fellowship. I think the Church far too often is an either/or church. Some churches are praising churches. This is the kind of church that places its emphasis on praise and worship. The church I pastor spends around one-fifth of its annual budget on praise and worship. We would definitely be a praising church. We love praise and we engage in praise. If you attend our church, you will know you are in a praising church. Some churches are Word churches. This is a church that is known for the way they preach and teach the Word of

God. The church I pastor spends about ¼ of its annual budget on the delivery of the Word. We are a church that is known for its preaching and teaching. I would say we are as known as much for one as we are for the other. Both worship and the Word are a priority to our church. Praise and preaching are partners. Worship and the Word are workers together in the service of the Lord. God never intended for these to be at odds with one another.

There are those churches that are not really defined by praise or by preaching. You would think this would be a rarity, but this is actually more common than the others. Think about your hometown and what the corner church in your town is identified by. I would guess most churches are identified by how social they are. Most smaller churches are known for being a family church. Some are known for being a particular family's church. A lot of smaller churches are small by design. They are much like the 80s TV show about a neighborhood bar. The show's theme song said,

Sometimes you want to go
Where everybody knows your name
And they're always glad you came
You want to be where you can see
The troubles are all the same
You want to be where everybody knows your name
(Gary Portnoy, Judy Hart Lyrics © Sony/ATV Music Publishing LLC)

These churches are built on this principle, and they are what they are by design.

It is hard for me to wrap my brain around this kind of thinking, but I have dealt with it even as a pastor of what I would consider a more progressive Pentecostal church for our area. I remember we once had a poor, white family who attended our church. They were not the caliber of people any church would naturally target. One of the ladies (who is no longer with us) said, "What are THEY doing here? Those people have their own churches." Never in all my years in church had I heard anyone tactfully verbalize that thought. Then, in my first year as pastor, we rented a very nice air-conditioned indoor pavilion on the river at the nicest park in the area for the 4th of July service. We had a planning meeting and went over the menu for the day. One of the ladies (also no longer with us) spoke up and said, 'We are not going to advertise that we have food. If we advertise that we have food, everyone will come." The statement took me by surprise. I thought that was the purpose. I wanted everyone to come. It was the first time I realized all the stories I heard about church people were true. We want to keep the church just like we like it. We want to know everyone and know everyone in our class of people. Let me go on record and say I refuse to be part of a church where not all people are welcome.

The larger churches are often known for the activities and social groups they provide. They almost become like a dozen smaller churches in one. They have a group for every age. This is not new, just repackaged. Years ago, when Sunday School was so big, every class was almost like a church within the church. When I first came to Lake City, there were three thriving adult

Sunday school classes. Each class kept the records of its membership. They had their accounts and planned their activities. Then, they came and joined everyone in the sanctuary for worship. Some left after Sunday School because Sunday School was their church. I remember one day being in a local grocery store and hearing a young man talking about his church. He was just praising his church. I thought how wonderful it was to hear a teenager so excited about his church. I knew I did not recognize the young man. I asked him where he attended church. He replied, "I am a No Limits youth group member." To my knowledge, he did not know me, and I did not know him, but he was a member of my church youth group. He did not say Lake City PH; he said No Limits. No Limits met in our gym, a whole other building away from the sanctuary. They did not have all the amenities we had in the main service. They were not exposed to the awesome worship the church paid dearly to have. None of those things brought this young man to our church. He came because that smaller group had become his family.

In reality, neither ministry of the Word nor ministry in music is behind the growth or continuation of a lot of larger churches. They are not dependent on great worship or great preaching for their growth. People are not there to hear powerful preaching or even outstanding singing. They have come for all the social benefits that come with the Church. They will bypass a church with great music if it satisfies their socialization needs. The question they are concerned about is, "What does this church offer my family? What do they have for my kids, for my teens, and for my marriage?" It can be really easy to feel these kinds of churches are no more than social clubs appealing to the human need for socialization.

The fact of the matter is that the New Testament Church was a church that understood the importance of fellowship. Right from the start of the New Testament Church, Acts Chapter 2 sets the tone for the New Testament Church to be an Engaging Church. Fellowship is a part of worship, and God loves for His children to fellowship. I am a father of three. My children are 13, 12, and 9 years old at the time of this writing. Most days, it is like World War III in our house. They are like three separate nations, each being a superpower, all at war with each other. On occasion, they all love each other. There is nothing like sitting in the living room and hearing them play together. Their laughter brings joy to my life. In fact, I would rather hear and see them playing together and loving each other than for them to hug and kiss me. As much as I love them telling me how good of a dad I am and how much they love me, I equally love them showing each other that love. I somehow believe this must be how God feels. It disappoints Him when we fuss and backstab each other. It brings joy to Him when He sees us loving each other and enjoying being together.

Over the years, I have been so driven by the ministry of the Word and having a good church that I have looked down on fellowship. I just wanted to have church all the time. I saw churches that were always having parties and social events as social clubs. Do not get me wrong; our main call is to provide a place of worship to our Lord and teach and train the saints. Our primary ministry is the Ministry of Reconciliation. This does not negate our need for fellowship. In my first youth pastorate, I was in my early 20s. I was young and zealous and saw the church headed in a direction away from God. I built our youth group around the church.

We had five services of some kind every week. We did Sunday School followed by morning worship. Sunday afternoon, we met at 4 pm, where I taught on the Book of Acts for 1 hour. Then, at 5 pm, we prayed for an hour, followed by Sunday night church at 6 pm. On Monday night, we met at 6 pm for a one-hour Bible study followed by prayer that could last till 9 pm or 10 pm. We met again on Wednesday at 7 pm for the youth class. Then, we had a full youth service every Friday night in our youth church. I remember my pastor's wife saying, "If you have church all the time and don't give kids a chance to play, they will eventually play church." Of course, I totally disagreed with that, but she was right. Those kids eventually did play church. As important as it is to have a good church, it is also important to have good fellowship.

It is built in us to fellowship. Think about the first conclusion the Bible gives to us concerning man. It is not good that man should be alone. Before sin is even introduced, the first thing God ever saw that was bad for man was for him to be alone. This need for fellowship is built in us. The need for the Church to provide for that need is built into it. On day one of the Church's life outside the Upper Room, the tone is set for the Church to be an Embracing Church. They started that day embracing one another. God knew, and Peter knew that strong fellowship makes for strong churches. A church with a strong core can survive anything thrown its way. God intended the Church to be a family. Whether you go to a small community church or a mega church, you should find a family in that church.

I grew up at the "T Street Church of God." My grandmother had moved her family to that church when they moved to the area when my mother was a young girl. My dad met my mom there, along with a lifetime of friends. When I was a child growing up, the T Street Church of God was my family. Even more to the point, the families of the T Street Church were my family. For the most part, my mom's family were not church-going people, even though they were raised in the Church. My grandfather lived to hunt, fish, and play golf. My grandmother lived for God. At that time, I learned that your spiritual family is more family to you than your blood family. It is wonderful when they can be the same, but sometimes that is not how it is. Though I greatly loved my grandfather, some of the older men in the church were more like grandfathers to me. Their families were my family. Their children were my aunts and uncles, and their grandchildren were my cousins.

Brother Z. T. Hodges was one of those men. I just knew him as Pop Hodges. We spent almost every Christmas at the Hodges' house. Though we had no blood relation to them, they were our family. Pops' oldest daughter was my mom's best friend. I knew her as my Aunt Martha; she was better to my brother and me than any blood aunt we ever had. When my grandmother was sick, and my mother had to stay around the clock with her mother, my Aunt Martha would drive a whole other town away to come to pick us up from school. She would then take us home, feed us, and care for us like her children. The day we buried my mother after I was already 50 years of age, my Aunt Martha wrapped her arms around my 46-year-old brother and me and said, "I do not just have two sons. I have four sons." These kinds of bonds will be formed in an embracing church that has learned how to love in deed and not just in word.

The Pitmans were another great T Street family. The T Street Church of God was started in the Pitman home nearly 100 years ago. When my grandmother was dying and had to be hospitalized for some time, Granny Pitman would cook for our family every Monday night so we could have a break from cancer and the hospital. I still remember those big yeast rolls Granny Pitman was so famous for. Her little house was a place of refuge in a time of storm. The day my grandmother passed, Granny Pittman came with enough food to feed an army. This was not the last time the Pitman family would be there for us. Fast forward the clock 35 years, and my mother is now the one dying. Granny Pitman has long been in the grave. Iris Pitman, the daughter-in-law of Granny Pitman, the niece-in-law of my Aunt Martha, and my mother's childhood friend of more than 70 years showed up for us. Iris practically moved into the house with us and stayed with my mother around the clock. She was there when Mom drew her last breath. She was with us through the funeral. On and on, I could go about the Hodges, the Pitmans, the Millers, and different pastors and stories of where our church family was there for us.

I write this section to show you what an embracing church looks like. The New Testament Church was not a Sunday experience. These people lived with each other, loved each other, and had all things in common. When one hurt, they all hurt; when one was blessed, they all were. The church must be about more than concerts and lectures. The church must even be about more than Bible studies. A true New

Testament Church does life together. This is more than just a modern catchphrase used by contemporary churches. This is something the New Testament Church embraced. Of course, they learned it from Jesus. Jesus spent 3½ years not only preaching and teaching but embracing those who were part of His family.

John 19:26-27, "When Jesus therefore saw His mother, and the disciple standing by, whom He loved, He saith unto His mother, Woman, behold thy son! Then saith He to the disciple, Behold thy mother! And from that hour, that disciple took her unto his own home."

Acts chapter 2 sets the tone for the New Testament Church to be an Embracing Church. The Scripture supports an Embracing Church. Traditional country churches did this long before the trendy churches ever thought of making it a catchphrase. These all did Life together. It was not a marketing campaign. This is something that happens when we are full of the Holy Ghost. The Holy Ghost produces love in our hearts for each other. The more of the Spirit we are filled with, the more of God's love we should be showing. There is a reason the old church referred to each other as brother and sister. There is a reason the church had church mothers. All of these are signs of being an embracing church. This should happen organically and not artificially. The church is not a test tube. The Church is a living, breathing organism made up of living tissue. This tissue is connected to other tissue, and the life of this tissue is dependent on its connection to that living tissue. This is why it is so vital that every Christian be connected to a local church and attend and support that local church faithfully. It is not enough to be a media church member. You need to be part of a local church and be present and accounted for in that church.

If you find yourself slipping in and out of church to avoid the drama, I get it. I understand church hurts. I understand why people come in and slip out, even with the understanding that you are missing out on one of the greatest aspects of the Church. There is no family like a church family. If you say, "My church is not embracing," I encourage you to be that agent of change in your church. Put yourself out there; I cannot promise you will not get hurt. I can promise if your church becomes a family, your children will have their own Hodges and Pitman families to write about. This does not happen through a marketed church service or church event. So much of what we do is like assigning seats to 1st graders. This embrace will naturally happen when the Spirit of God is at work in the hearts of God's people.

Acts Chapter 2 does give us instructions on how this embrace happens. First, they bore each other's burdens. It's hard to root for someone to succeed if their failure will cost you. Secondly, they went to church often and worshiped God together. It is like the old saying: the family that prays together stays together. Thirdly, they ate together at each other's houses. This may not be applicable for today, but we can eat out. Every Sunday, we should eat out or invite people over. There is a powerful bond that is formed when we eat together and do it often. Our Conference Council recently took a trip together. We traveled together, we worshiped together, we ate together, and we laughed together. Eating, laughing, praying, and worshiping together will create a spiritual bond in the family of God. We are stronger together; it is time we embrace each other as the family God intended us to be.

1 Corinthians 12:20-25, "But now are they many members, yet but one body. And the eye cannot say unto the hand, I have no need of thee: nor again the head to the feet, I have no need of you. Nay, much more those members of the body, which seem to be more feeble, are necessary: And those members of the body, which we think to be less honorable, upon these we bestow more abundant honor; and our uncomely parts have more abundant comeliness. For our comely parts have no need: but God hath tempered the body together, having given more abundant honor to that part which lacked. That there should be no schism in the body, but that the members should have the same care one for another."

Chapter 8:

"The Church Of Acts Was An Evolving Church"

Acts 2:47, "Praising God, and having favor with all the people. And <u>the Lord added to the church daily such as should be saved.</u>"

As we start this final chapter, I want to ensure we are not thrown off by the word "evolving". To evolve has a connotation of moving from its origin. In this case I mean that we are evolving back to our origin. In no way am I talking about a church that is evolving in the means of morality. As one famous TV preacher said when asked about his view on homosexuality, "It has evolved and is evolving." When I say that Acts chapter 2 set the tone for the New Testament Church to be an Evolving Church, this does not apply to morality. We cannot afford for our views on sin to evolve. The New Testament is the moral authority, and what the New Testament clearly calls sin is sin. All sexual sin has been exposed in the New Testament. There is no wiggle room concerning sexual sin. On the subject of sexual sin, the

Bible could not be more precise. Any evolution on these subjects would be a clear rejection of God's Holy Word.

1 Corinthians 6:9-11, "Know ye not that the unrighteous shall not inherit the Kingdom of God? Be not deceived: neither fornicators, nor idolaters, nor adulterers, nor effeminate, nor abusers of themselves with mankind, Nor thieves, nor covetous, nor drunkards, nor revilers, nor extortioners, shall inherit the Kingdom of God. And such were some of you: but ye are washed, but ye are sanctified, but ye are justified in the name of the Lord Jesus, and by the Spirit of our God."

When I use the term evolving, I am using the term in the sense of growing and moving forward and expanding our understanding of the Scripture. Progressive has become a term to describe the most immoral and Godless among us. The Democrats talk about the progressive wing of their party. When the media uses this description, they are referring to the members of that Party who are in full agreement with the most extreme abortion rights. This is where a child can be executed right up to – and in some cases, even after – birth. This term is applied to those who feel parents should have no say in their children's decisions concerning the mutilation of their bodies. Of course, they call this "gender realignment". The Progressive wing is speaking of those who fully support the Palestinians over the Jews. When they use the term "progressive", they are speaking to the very core of an anti-Christian, anti-Jewish, non-Biblical worldview. When I speak of "progression", I simply mean moving forward in God's Word and God's plan for man.

The Church has never been called to entertain sin or rethink sin. The Church must draw a line of demarcation. The Church must declare righteousness and holiness to this unholy world. The Church cannot be ambiguous; it must be clear on all positions to which the Bible clearly speaks. Paul tells us in the 2nd Book of Corinthians, the 13th chapter, that in the mouth of two or three witnesses, let it be established. When the Bible speaks to something multiple times, it brings clarity that cannot be ignored or twisted. Holiness is still right, sin is still wrong, and Jesus will always be Lord. May the Church make a clear statement as to where it stands on these issues. People may not like where we stand, but they should know where we stand. The New Testament Church must be a Church of conviction. If we are anchored and rooted in and to the Word of God, we will never have to be worried about evolving or progressing to the place where we no longer reassemble the New Testament Church. No matter how far we may progress, we are attached to an unmovable reference point called the BIBLE, the Word of God. His Word is the first and final word on any subject concerning morality and spirituality.

On the Day of Pentecost, the Church was in its infancy. It was a newborn baby with a lot of growing to do. The New Covenant, as we know, was still being discovered. Over 20 years later, the Apostle Paul would take his place as an outstanding leader of the New Testament Church. It would be several years after this that Paul would write his letters to the Churches. We have more than 6½ decades from the Day of Pentecost until John would write the Book of Revelation, and possibly even longer than that before we would have the Gospel of John. So even the doctrine of the New Testament was in a state of evolving on the Day of Pentecost. Over the next decades, the Church would come to understand the fullness of God's plan, but they certainly did not have it all on that day.

On the day of Pentecost, what they did have in hand were the Old Testament Scriptures. They relied heavily on those and on the Holy Ghost to reveal understanding of those texts. Even their understanding of the Old Testament was evolving. They also had the words and actions of Jesus. Peter would later write they were eyewitnesses of these words and actions. On the Day of Pentecost, they did not even have a single written sentence of a single Gospel. By the end of the day on the Day of Pentecost, they had put together enough information that by the power of the Holy Spirit, they had what they called the Apostle's Doctrine. This doctrine was evolving because of the revelation of the

Holy Spirit. These early Apostles gave themselves completely to prayer and studying the Hebrew Scriptures. Through this prayer and study, God gave the same divine revelation to these nine men as He did to the thirty-one who penned the Old Testament.

The understanding of this Doctrine and its audience was in a state of evolution. When they first started preaching, they only preached to fellow Jews. Peter had read and preached what Joel had written but did not understand it. They all knew what John the Baptist had said about God raising up children unto Abraham out of stones. Though they knew what he said and probably quoted it, they did not understand it. Have you ever read a passage a half dozen times, but on the 7th time, a light came on? Even our understanding of the Bible is in constant evolution. Even though they had the Book of Joel and the prophecy of John, they still missed it. With his mouth, Peter said this power is available to ALL flesh, but in his actions, he withheld grace from anyone who was not born a Jew.

This reminds me of how the Church in America operated and, sadly, in some places still operates. They say with their mouths and in their preaching that this unspeakable gift is for everyone, but then they reserve it only for a certain class. Many, especially in the South where I live, love missions. They love black and brown children in Africa and Central America, but despise black and brown children in America. When we bypass a community or mistreat people who come to our church because of the color of their skin, we are doing what the early Church did. For most of you reading this book, if you and I had lived in that time, we would have been those from whom the Gospel would have been withheld. Thank God for those who love everyone. This Gospel is for every person of every color. This Gospel is for divorced people looking for God. How many divorced people has the Church withheld the Gospel from in the past 100 years? This Gospel is for homosexuals who are fed up with their sin and desire to be set free. God loves the homosexual. He does not love homosexuality, but He loves the one trapped in that sin and expects His Church to preach the chain-breaking Gospel to them.

There is no sexual sin that has disqualified anyone from receiving the grace of God and being born again. I am thankful that most of the churches have evolved past prejudice and open their arms to all. I am also grateful that we can love people in the process. This Gospel is not for perfect people; it is for whoever will come to the Lord. Through the Gospel, and the Holy Spirit's work of sanctification we are in the process of perfection.

The New Testament Church went almost seven years following this pattern of only preaching to Jewish people. It was in Acts 8 that a great expansion of thought took place. Here, they find themselves in Samaria, and the Samaritans receive the Gospel. This is truly a shame that it took this long for this evolution to take place. Almost a decade earlier, Peter and the other disciples – who, by this time, are now leaders of the New Testament Church – were with Jesus when He encountered that now famous woman at the well. You would have thought any of them would have spoken up and said, "JESUS LOVES SAMARITANS!!!" These men would have witnessed how the whole town showed up to see Jesus, how Jesus embraced them, and how they embraced Him. Personal prejudice and bigoted bias are powerful things. These are tools of the flesh, and they work against the acceleration of the Church. This is something the Church of Acts would have to fight for 100 years. In reality, it is something we still fight today, but I thank God for the progress we have made and the progress we are making.

Jesus encountered a blind man in need of sight. Jesus touched the man, and he saw men as trees. From the start of man's productivity, trees have been a vital resource. We use them to build houses and all sorts of structures. We use them to make paper and we use paper for more things than I can mention. When Jesus touched this man and saw men as trees, I believe there was a revelation revealed that the modern church needs to hear. We need to see men as men and not as trees. Too many churches only see people as a resource, a resource to support their programs. People are placed in a category of assets and liabilities. We keep the assets and get rid of the liabilities. We, like this blind man, need another touch of the Master's hand until we see people are people and they are all valuable in the sight of both God and the Church.

A decade after Pentecost and three years after the Samaritan revival, God had to deal with Peter dramatically. At this time, God shows Peter a sheet lowered down with all the animals Peter had been taught not to eat. Then an evolution he never expected took place in his life. This is an evolution that would change not only Peter, but the trajectory of the entire New Testament Church. God commanded Peter to rise and eat. Peter is appalled and argues with God over His command. Peter thinks he is too holy to obey God. It is foolishness and the height of arrogance when we believe we know better than God. This is an argument we will never win. Just ask John the Baptist when he thought he knew better than Jesus on who should baptize who. We often cloak our disagreement with God in holiness and humility. There is no acceptable reason to disagree with God. This is what religious traditions often do. In their perceptions, they become a higher authority than the Spirit or Scripture. So often, churches have been locked into a bad past due to tradition. The famous last words of a church are, "We have never done it this way before."

Any tradition that keeps us from or hinders our worship is a bad tradition. Churches have been locked into bad, non-Biblical, and even anti-Biblical traditions. These traditions have kept them from properly praising God and reaching people. This is what Peter and the New Testament Church dealt with in the first decade of the New Testament Church. A people a thousand times greater in number than the Jews had been bypassed over Jewish tradition and a faulty understanding of God's plan. I would dare say the Church of today still has some evolving to do when it comes to praising God and reaching people. The good news is that we have made great evolutionary leaps forward in both areas. May our traditions no longer hinder us from praising God and reaching people. May the Holy Spirit be our guide, as He was the guide of the New Testament Church. We are not perfect, and the New Testament Church did not start perfect. It took evolution through the Holy Spirit and the work of sanctification to bring them to a place of perfect submission.

The New Testament Church had evolved to a place where they reached out to everyone. The New Testament still had to evolve in their understanding of the New Covenant. By the time the New Testament had been written, the Church was walking in the knowledge of the New Covenant. Paul was given great revelation. Evangelist Jimmy Swaggart says Paul was given the New Covenant. Paul and the other New Testament writers placed these revaluations in a perfect book which we call the New Testament. The New Testament, like the Old Testament, is perfect. It is the inspired, infallible Word of God and is perfect. What is not perfect is our understanding of all that has been written. There is an evolution that has taken place, and it is taking place concerning that understanding.

Ephesians 4:13, "Till we all come in the unity of the faith, and of the knowledge of the Son of God, unto a perfect man, unto the measure of the stature of the fulness of Christ:"

Through the years, much of the understanding of the New Covenant and the plan of God had been lost in Catholicism and tradition. Through the Holy Spirit, God began to bring evolution and revolution to His Church over the years. Due to the hostile takeover of the organized church by the Roman Empire, much of the revelation was lost. The Bible was written in a language very few people, even the clergy, could read. The Bible was chained to pulpits and kept away from the people. They were told they could not understand it anyway. The organized church became a place where man's thoughts trumped the Word of God until the Word of God became a memory. As one Jesuit priest said, "The more I read this Book (the Bible), the more I realize it is against us (Catholicism)." With this thinking, no wonder the great works of God were lost to the Church.

God would not allow His Church to remain in darkness, so He started to bring about revelation. The revelation would bring the Church back into a state of evolution after 1,000 years of darkness. I want you to picture a powerful light bulb sitting on a desk. I want you to see a man come in and cover that powerful light with a slat box. Looking at this box, you can see light escaping through the sides of these slats. The slats have blocked the light's fullness, but cannot contain the light. This light is the Gospel of Christ, the Apostles' Doctrine, and the fullness of the New Covenant. This slat box is both Catholic and religious tradition. This box cannot contain or conceal all the light. There is enough light escaping from the box that countless millions of souls over a thousand years saw the light and were saved. Many saw enough of the light that they walked in much of the revelation. Yet the vast majority of the revelation was concealed from most people.

Around 1517, God moved on a man named Martin Luther. Martin Luther, a German Priest, took the crowbar of God's Word, walked over to the slat box, and removed the center slat. He read a straightforward verse of God's pure Word: the just shall live by faith. With this reading, he nailed to the door of the Wittenberg Castle Church his "95 Theses". The nail hitting the door of this church was the shot heard around the world. It also reverberated throughout the spirit realm. The light came pouring out of the box, and from the light, the revelation of salvation by faith was restored to the Church. We take it for granted but imagine the wonders of knowing that your sins are forgiven due to faith in Jesus. For 1,000 years, man had been working for his own salvation. Most of this work involved making the Pope and Rome richer and richer. Now we understand that Christ lived good enough for all of us. If we place our hope and trust in His life, His death, and in His resurrection, we are saved by faith through grace.

Hundreds of years go by, and the light of grace is brightly shining. People are still living and struggling with how they can please God. Grace for salvation is clear, but the holiness needed for a life pleasing to God seems to be out of their reach. All they have ever known are the rules of religion that shackled them for a thousand years. So, with these rules, they do their very best to try to please God. Then God raised up a mighty man full of faith and the Word to take the crowbar of the Bible and remove another slat. John Wesley began preaching and teaching the doctrine of Sanctification. Through the power of the Holy Spirit, we can die in the flesh and have the Spirit of Christ resurrected in us. It was the removal of this slat that brought the Church into an evolution that brought about Biblical Holiness. We are now able to please God through the intentions of a pure heart and not the keeping of man-made rules.

In the late 1800s, God handed His crowbar to another man. This was a man by the name of Charles Fox Parham. Charles Parham noticed a pattern in the Book of Acts concerning the reception of the Holy Ghost. He noted that when people were baptized in the Holy Spirit, they spoke with other tongues. It was from this teaching that Charles Fox Parham pulled the slat off the box, and the light of the Baptism of the Holy Ghost came pouring out for all to see. This was an evolution that did not just unlock one Biblical truth but opened up the Church to a world of Spiritual power. Now, we have access to all the gifts of the Spirit. If Charles Fox Parham gave us the spark of Pentecost, William J. Seymour poured a bucket of gasoline over that flame. This evolution at the Azusa Street Mission has brought the Church into an age of power.

It has been said that the Book of Acts has no closing. It has also been said we are currently living in Acts chapter 29. This is not to say that the Bible is being added to. When the canon was closed, the door of all Biblical inspiration was closed. No prophet can add to or take away from this Bible. What is not closed off are the wonderful Holy Ghost revelations about Holy Scripture. The New Testament Church was a church on fire. Acts chapter 2 set the tone for the Church of Acts to be an Evolving Church. We should be evolving today. We should be evolving in new ways of reaching the lost. We should develop new wineskins and mechanisms to get the pure wine of God's revelation to the world. If we grow in grace and holiness together, we will not be liberal or legalistic. If we hold to the unchanging Scriptures, we can evolve in power and not be a space cadet. An Evolving Church is not a liberal church, nor is it a conservative church. An Evolving Church is a Biblical Church, evolving in grace, holiness, and power.

Acts 28:30-31, "And Paul dwelt two whole years in his own hired house, and received all that came in unto him, Preaching the Kingdom of God, and teaching those things which concern the Lord Jesus Christ, with all confidence, no man forbidding him."

Made in the USA
Middletown, DE
11 May 2025

75376863R00106